W9-ACG-897

FOUNDERS OF MODERN EGYPT

FOUNDERS OF MODERN EGYPT

MARY ROWLATT

Foreword by

DR. G. P. GOOCH, O.M.

ASIA PUBLISHING HOUSE

BOMBAY . CALCUTTA . NEW DELHI . MADRAS
LONDON . NEW YORK

PRINTED IN INDIA
BY Z. T. BANDUKWALA AT LEADERS PRESS
PRIVATE LIMITED, BOMBAY AND PUBLISHED BY P. S.
JAYASINGHE, ASIA PUBLISHING HOUSE, BOMBAY-1

FOREWORD

THIS book is a genuine contribution to history, for it tells the story of memorable events from the inside. Its theme is the birth of Egyptian nationalism in the last quarter of the nineteenth century which is inseparably connected with the name of Arabi. Owing to her geographical position at the junction of two Continents, Egypt has always played a significant part in the development of events. Cairo is as much in the news today as ever, and Nasser has fulfilled the ambitions which led Egyptian patriots to shed their blood eighty years ago. Thus, though the narrative ends with the battle of Tel al Kebir in 1882, the surrender of Arabi, and the inauguration of the British Occupation under the prudent guidance of Lord Cromer, there is a breath of actuality in these pages.

Miss Rowlatt is exceptionally well equipped for her task, since her grandfather spent his later years in Egypt, her father was born there, and she herself grew up speaking Arabic as well as English. The curtain rises on the spendthrift Khedive Ismail in whose reign the Suez Canal was opened in 1869, whose ever mounting debts cost him the throne ten years later. His thoughtless sacrifice of his country's interests led to two serious consequences. Firstly a group of Egyptian patriots, military and civilian, declined to remain idle spectators of a rake's progress. Secondly, British bondholders, realising the uselessness of diplomatic protests, resorted to arms when anarchy and bankruptcy stared the country in the face. The British fleet bombarded Alexandria, occupied the capital after the verdict of the stricken field. Ismail had been succeeded as Khedive by his colourless son Tewfik, who had at first cooperated with Arabi, his war minister, in an attempt to rescue the country from the morass into which Ismail had plunged it; but the happy partnership was soon terminated by personal rivalry. Both were patriots, but they and their respective supporters differed as to who was to run the country. The British military intervention, which caused John Bright to resign from the Gladstone Cabinet, found a certain justification in their contention that they were upholding the authority of the Khedive and saving Egypt from civil war. The situation had been further complicated by the non-military intervention of the Sultan of Turkey, who preferred the timid Tewfik to the dynamic Minister of War. All these exciting events are illustrated in the contemporary correspondence of the author's family in which are mirrored the hopes and fears, the ambitions and intrigues of the principal actors on the crowded stage. The most novel feature in the book, next to the family letters, is the full length portrait of Mohammed Abdu, the spiritual leader of Egyptian nationalism, about whose activities English readers have hitherto known little or nothing. Arabi, whose reforming zeal he shared, comes out on the whole well in these pages, but it is always easier for a thinker than a man of action to keep his name untarnished. Mazzini was never exposed to the temptations which assailed Cavour.

Egyptian nationalism and the Moslem world had a devoted and influential friend in Wilfrid Blunt, poet and publicist. It was owing to him that the services of Broadley, an English barrister, were secured for the trial of Arabi, and when the exile was allowed to return to Egypt in broken health after many years the friendship was renewed, for Blunt possessed a hospitable house near Cairo. Even closer were Blunts personal ties with Abdu, who had received a short term of banishment for his association with Arabi. Abdu, unlike Arabi, was a man of wide culture, who desired to learn what Europe could teach without abandoning the foundations of his Moslem faith. In his later years he decided to learn French, visited Blunt in his Sussex home, and made the acquaintance of some prominent English politicians. Abdu lived to become a judge under the British occupation, and to be revered by all who knew him. What nobler career can be conceived than that of a builder of bridges between different continents, races and faiths?

G. P. GOOCH o.m.

AUTHOR'S NOTE

IN the course of this book I have often quoted directly from original records rather than re-phrase them. This has been consciously done for it is a chapter of history the details of which are so little remembered that accurate information and exact contemporary views are frequently needed. Thus the tale is told largely but not wholly through the medium of the author.

At the same time it is a chapter of history so peopled with interesting characters that to keep the thread of the tale intact, it has been impossible to enlarge on them all. Of such are Abdullah Nadim, the gifted propagandist; "Abu Naddara", the journalist; Mahmoud Sami and the Prime Ministers, Riyad and Sherif. The same is true of some events, such as the functioning of the Chamber of Notables and the rise of the popular Egyptian press.

For the sake of consistency I have occasionally altered the English spelling of Arabic names when quoting from other writers, so as to avoid the same place or the same person reappearing in a confusing variety of forms. But I have not done so where the title of a book is concerned.

M. R.

ACKNOWLEDGMENTS

I wish to thank the Librarians of the Royal Commonwealth Society, and of the School of Oriental and African Studies, London, for permission to use these fine libraries; also the Librarians and staffs of the Royal Institute of International Affairs, the Royal Asiatic Society and the Royal Central Asian Society for patient and effective co-operation in finding source material.

Special thanks are due to Messrs. Savory and Moore for permission to publish passages from their nineteenth century business correspondence; to the Keeper of Italian Naval Archives, Rome, for kindly verifying relevant details; to Miss Coates, the Registrar of the National Register of Archives, London, for valuable help in securing original documents; to Dr. A. al Batrik, Cultural Counsellor to the United Arab Republic Embassy, London and to Mr. M. M. Harouni, lately of The United Arab Republic Education Bureau, London, for welcome help with Arabic material.

I am also grateful to the Editor of the *Contemporary Review* for permission to quote from an article of mine originally published in that journal. And finally I wish to thank Miss Marjorie Procter for invaluable help in proof-reading.

M. R.

CONTENTS

Illustrations between pages 80-81

PART I

THE STAGE IS SET—1866-1881

CHAPTER I

INTRODUCTORY

THIS book tells the tale of a crucial scene in Anglo-Egyptian history, culminating in the British military occupation of 1882.

From among the varied participants in this scene two are here chosen as chief actors—Ahmed Arabi, the soldier, and Mohammed Abdu, the thinker, who played vital parts in the creating of Egyptian nationalism. Thought and action in the United Arab Republic of today are affected by the lives of these two men.

It was the latter half of the nineteenth century that also saw the significant rise of Indian nationalism. In 1885 the Indian National Congress was started on the initiative of an Englishman, Allan Octavian Hume. Sheikh Mohammed Abdu was well aware of these Indian developments and he also drew inspiration from the teachings of the great Indian reformer Sayed Ahmed Khan.

As the rising led by Ahmed Arabi gathered momentum it was backed in spirit by a considerable body of Indian opinion. So much so that the British government decided to circulate in India the proclamation which eventually denounced Arabi as a rebel.

This book has not been written to point out that Britain was right or wrong to have become involved in Egyptian affairs towards the end of the last century with force of arms and force of gold. But it does suggest that the thinking and motives behind the way in which she was involved resulted in an oppression of people's characters and personalities, and an oppression of that nebulous, delicate thing, which is the budding of a nation's personality.

The story of those years is tragedy. One has the sense of fate engulfing the actors, carrying them to conclusions none of them wished for, at tremendous cost. And at the same time one senses that it need not have happened. One sees a pattern of relationships inexorably emerging—a pattern that has repeated itself in many other situations and countries where we British have gone since; where domination and mistrust have frustrated Britain's best work and effort, until she carries such an overhead of hatred that she can no longer give what she needs to give and could. To break the chain of fate and create a fresh pattern needs radical re-thinking of every assumption, and above all of every superiority.

3

Many British who have forgotten the story of those early years in Egypt, express their opinions freely about the Egypt of today, and feel totally at a loss to understand why good will and gratitude are not in the ascendant, and from where the hatred has come.

It is common experience in the lives of individual people that a man who finds himself in grave difficulties may have to go back to events of years before, see what was wrong in them, and as far as possible, set it right. He may be unconscious of any original mistakes, merely hopelessly frustrated by the breakdown and division and ineffectiveness of living, in which, however hard he tries, the same pattern re-appears, often with the people he loves most.

The alternative to rupture in such cases can be, and often is, some re-birth of the spirit which enables the man to see, in a new perspective, the deep hurts and smouldering resentments he has caused. Things he had thought irrelevant and of no importance suddenly take their place as sources of poison needing cure, and honesty opens the way to healing and a fresh start.

Hatred and love are very close together. The most violent feelings come between those who actually need each other and are bound together by common tasks and common urgencies. The same may be true of nations.

This story of Ahmed Arabi, Mohammed Abdu and the birth of Egyptian nationalism could be one such turning point in our history. If so, it is well worth the effort of thought and honesty to see what went right and what went wrong, what other people felt about it as well as what Britain felt herself, where pettiness fogged statesmanship and blindness missed essentials. All could be clues as to how nations of our day, amid our choices, can forge a new pattern of relationships, wherein all concerned can find a new greatness, relevant to the age in which we live.

CHAPTER II

THE SETTING OF THE SCENE

"TAKE care as you descend the grand staircase," said the Khedive Ismail to a departing American guest, "if you slip you risk falling on the Nilotic Hydra with ten heads which rise again as you cut them off." The Khedive counted on his fingers, "A consul, a go-between, a scoundrel, a journalist, a count, a baron, a financier, a money-forger, a Greek and an Armenian."[1]

If this is not a tape-recorded conversation it is at least an impressionist picture in which caricature plays but the smallest part.

The Khedive Ismail ruled Egypt from 1863 to 1879. He was the grandson of Mohammed Ali, the Albanian Turk who founded Egypt's latest ruling dynasty, and he was the grandfather of Farouk, the last of that dynasty to rule. In Ismail's day, Egypt being still part of the Turkish empire meant that in spite of the Khedive's sovereign powers in many respects, a yearly tribute had to be paid to the Sultan in Constantinople who was the final arbiter in some Egyptian matters of state, such as the size of the army and the conferring of high-ranking titles.

Ismail's financial affairs were conducted on a large scale. In 1866 he purchased from the Sultan the right to nominate his eldest son to the Egyptian throne; this innovation cost him many thousands of pounds. In 1869 he was host to one of the most spectacular gatherings ever held of nineteenth century crowned heads to celebrate the opening of the Suez Canal. This cost him millions more. By now he had acquired for his own use about a sixth of all cultivatable land in Egypt, which somewhat off-set his expenses. In 1873 he obtained further privileges from the Sultan, including the right to coin money and to make treaties with foreign powers; but the Sultan raised the annual tribute due to the Porte, till it reached the sum of 133,635 purses, equivalent to about £681,550. In 1874 Ismail sold 176,602 of his shares in the Suez Canal Company to England, so drained of money had he become. This was the dramatic moment when Disraeli, with the help of the House of Rothschild, was able to raise £3,976,582 on the spot, cash down, in exchange for the shares.

[1] See *Arabi Pasha* by J. Ninet. Privately printed, St. Quentin, 1884, p. 280.

5

6 6   FOUNDERS OF MODERN EGYPT

Debt after debt had been contracted with European Powers but the personal extravagances of Ismail and his entourage were still fabulous. One of his Princesses had run up a bill of £150,000 with a French dressmaker. In some instances huge bills went unpaid and in other cases unscrupulous contractors not only over-charged Ismail, but managed to extract the full over-charge. The harbour works at Alexandria were in that category. They cost over £2,500,000 but a trustworthy estimate of the day shows that they should have cost £1,400,000. [2]

Although it is true that Ismail in person was much to blame for the situation, it is also true that he was surrounded by rapacious and flattering Europeans who had but one thing in common— bright ideas on the spending of Ismail's money in such a way as to transfer it from his pocket to theirs. Barons of dubious lineage, titled racketeers, and plausible inventors with plans for the furthering of their own inventions, milled round the court in their dozens and there never lacked a banking establishment ready to lend the Khedive still more money at still higher rates of interest.

Yet Ismail was no fool in many ways. Though caught in the trap of his own making, he often saw through the characteristics of those who hurried round to make the best of it, as they helped to fasten him all the more securely within that trap.

So much European money was sunk in this financial nightmare that the Powers were convinced that the bond-holders should be protected. As far as England was concerned it could be said that one main consideration took precedence over the financial one. "The leading aim of our policy in Egypt," wrote Lord Salisbury, "is the maintenance of the neutrality of that country, that is to say the maintenance of such a state of things that no great Power shall be more powerful there than England." [3] The word "neutrality" had a somewhat different content for Lord Salisbury then, than for President Nasser now.

The day of financial reckoning drew near and Ismail, under pressure from Europe, eventually allowed an international committee of inquiry to be formed whose business was to clarify the well-nigh bankrupt state of his government and of his personal affairs. The Englishman nominated to this, in 1877, was an artillery officer—

[2] See *Modern Egypt* by The Earl of Cromer, Macmillan, 1911, p. 40.
[3] Lord Salisbury, Minister of Foreign Affairs to Mr. Malet, 16 October 1879. Public Records Office, F.O. 78/2997.

Major Baring—who later, as Lord Cromer, was to play so large a part in the reconstruction of modern Egypt. To unravel the complications, the waste and the trickery was a task indeed. Day after day of concentrated work in a hot Egyptian summer threw some light on the unbelievable transactions that had taken place, but how certain large sums had been dissipated remains a mystery to this day.

The man who suffered most from this state of things was the man who least deserved to suffer—the Egyptian peasant. One Englishman who was able to see this for himself was my maternal grandfather, J. E. Cornish. In January 1871 he went to Egypt to recover from a serious illness. After a couple of months in Upper Egypt his health had so much improved that he was about to return to England. But on the way back, while in Cairo, he was introduced to Ismail: "I found him an exceedingly shrewd individual", wrote my grandfather, "although he had at that time transacted personally an immense amount of business, he liked to meet people. He was always keen to see if he could turn any man's wits to his own account".

Ismail asked my grandfather if he wished to remain in the country, if so, although he had as many engineers as he wanted, he would find him some small post. The result was that Cornish remained in Ismail's service for nearly four years; many subsequent years in Egypt were to follow. On looking back to those four years, 1871 to 1875, my grandfather considered it was then that Ismail sowed the seeds of which the harvest was reaped in 1882.

On his way to join the works in Upper Egypt, for which he was engaged, Cornish saw for himself the system of forced labour or "corvée". The better to irrigate the vast acres of land which Ismail had acquired unto himself he proceeded to make a new canal (the present Ibrahimia). Although intended to irrigate only his own lands it was entirely made by "corvée". That is to say the workmen received no pay or anything else beyond just enough hard biscuit to keep body and soul together. The ground followed close to the railway on which my grandfather travelled south so he was able to see that for some 130 miles it was covered with men as close as they could work together. He was told that there were about 60,000 working on it at the same time.

During his stay in Upper Egypt he was at different times in charge of the erection or working of three large sugar factories. These were visited frequently by Ismail himself. His emissaries came from Cairo to the officials and even to mosques and markets, to explain to the people, that some very erroneous notions had got about in recent lax times with reference to property in land, which really all belonged to the Khedive who could take it when he liked, and who would give in return an equal area of land in another place. It was generally found that these other places were on the borders of the desert or land remote from water.

Some landowners refused to give up their property without a struggle. These were generally visited by a party of Government officials whose arguments, combined with a free use of the whip, usually settled the matter. Some of the more obdurate were imprisoned on one pretext or another, and others were sent to the White Nile, a place from which the traveller in those days was hardly expected to return.

All the men working on Ismail's sugar factories had their names written down on pay sheets, but the pay day seemed to be indefinitely postponed. My grandfather concluded that the principal object in keeping these pay sheets was to see whether the men were there or not, so that they might be duly punished if they absented themselves.

All these arrangements were kept as much as possible from the knowledge of the foreign technical staff and any questions only elicited evasive answers. Such happenings could not be carried on without giving rise to some grumbling, and it began to be whispered that complaints had been made to various Consuls-General in Cairo. Ismail, it was said, had been told that his affairs were not being run as befitted a Member of the Society for the Abolition of Slavery. The Khedive Ismail had joined this Society during his visit to London in 1864. He had stayed with the Duke of Sutherland at Stafford House who was a keen supporter of the Society.

One of the results of these complaints was that orders came from Cairo that the men working on the factories were actually to be paid. Money was sent, and for some time they were paid though this was not an unmixed blessing, for Ismail became much more exacting as to the amount of work they had to do. Many officers of his guard, and other military men of high position, were stationed around the different works to see that no time was lost.

My grandfather, being of a friendly disposition, became well-known to some of these officers, in spite of the tiresome circumstances in which they met.

In the early part of 1874 a rapid decline set in on the tide of Ismail's affairs. Nearly all the new works in hand were stopped, and no money could be found for the proper working of the older factories. My grandfather Cornish was in charge of a sugar factory, the workmen of which had not been paid for eight months, when an order came from Cairo that they were to be paid in molasses. It so happened that the molasses had been lying in open tanks for several months.

When writing about his experiences of the time, J. E. Cornish says expressly that he refers to only a few of the many cases which during four years came under his observation, all tending to show an almost tyrannous oppression on the one hand, and ill-concealed resentment on the other. He came to the conclusion that this must end badly, and early in 1874 made up his mind to leave the country as soon as he conveniently could. Fate, however, decreed otherwise and in 1878 he was back again in Egypt.[4]

While my maternal grandfather Cornish was wrestling with the sugar factories and the unfortunate Egyptian peasants who manned them, my paternal grandfather Rowlatt was manager of the Bank of Egypt in Alexandria.

He had his worries too, but has only left in writing a laconic flavour of those difficult days, in his letters to his wife. "I came back having seen the Khedive about the £160,000," he writes. "I had to wait two and a half hours in an antechamber before seeing him. I would not be a courtier for £5000 a year. . . . They say the Khedive is to give lots of balls this winter and therefore dissipation and gaiety of all kinds, I suppose, will be rampant in Cairo. . . . Do you remember the 'Countess' and her husband we met one evening? Well it seems that they are regular swindlers. Another proof of the necessity of avoiding all countesses."

". . . The Viceroy [one of Ismail's styles], it seems, is in a dreadful state of mind. What he called the 'Judicial reforms', they say, are quite gone to pot—and also the succession arrangements. . . . They say the Viceroy has spent £2,000,000 in this affair, and *all for nothing*."

Another picture, so far unpublished, of Ismail's days and ways,

---

[4] My Cornish grandfather's reminiscences of these years were privately printed in a pamphlet in 1909 and circulated among friends. A short extract of some ten lines was used by Charles Royle in his book, *The Egyptian Campaigns* 1882-1885. Hurst and Blackett, 1886, Vol. 1, pp. 194-5.

has recently come to light from an unexpected source. It appears that Ismail had lodged an order with Messrs. Savory and Moore, the London chemists, for a series of private pharmacies attached to his palaces and to his royal yacht.

A certain Mr. Dispenser Bateman was in charge of the venture, which started in 1874. His correspondence with Savory and Moore in London throws many amusing and some pathetic sidelights on the reactions of a mid-Victorian chemist and his wife to Ismail, his court and his ways. The Khedive's affability impressed him much: "Yesterday His Highness drove past me, and as soon as he saw me he stopped his carriage, *jumped out* and asked me how I was, and if I were contented with what had been done. I answered: 'Oui Monsignor'. . . . I have received seven invitations to breakfast and dine with His Highness so I know he is satisfied with the working of his Pharmacy and the other day he told me personally that I might take my wife with me to Ghizeh Palace where we are expected to move any day."

It was not long, however, before this highly respected firm realised that things were not always here conducted in a manner to which they were accustomed. They next learnt that gentle hints on the payment of bills and salaries were of no avail.

By 1876 the London office wrote to Mr. Bateman:". . . Unless, it seems to me, we *insist* upon having the previous claim settled at once the amount will be allowed to reach £5000 before next summer. I am quite sure that we shall succeed in this object by constantly applying and dunning the authorities and even bringing the case to the notice of H.H. if we cannot very shortly obtain payment. . . . In the shipment of last week we sent 12 doz. boxes of Quinine pills, which I want you to shew to H.H. or any other personage you think best, with the proposal that we shall send about 25,000 of these pills in similar boxes for the use of the Troops of His Highness who are engaged in the war with Turkey—I mean as a gift to the sick and wounded. They are pills that we made for the French Army and are as good as at first. (You need not, of course, make any allusion to this fact.) You may be able, in putting forward this offer, to give a lift to the money question as well—that you will see. . . ."

The conducting of affairs was by no means easy for Mr. Dispenser Bateman. It appears that the head Hareem doctor had come across some toothpicks among the stores sent to Cairo by Savory and Moore.

He got it into his head that these were meant as a present for himself and complained that it was paltry, not even being made of silver. "Well, after a little chat," wrote Mr. Bateman, "it came out that he wanted a dressing-bag—a small one such as he could carry about in his hand. As this man is in a position to do much harm if he likes to the pharmacy—I thought I would propose that you should send me one out for him—it can be charged as Quinine or some such drug if you like. I would suggest one something like Mappin & Webb's with silver engine—turned tops—their price is about £5.5.0."

Some political comment enters the correspondence:

"I have been glad to see by the speech of Mr. Cross, Home Secretary, that H.M.'s Government do intend to watch over Egypt, the Canal, Constantinople, Dardanelles and Bosphorus, so that those brutes of Russians will have to keep their distance from those parts. I hope this will reassure the Khedive and bring about a more comfortable state of matters financial than has existed there for a long time. Nothing could be worse than the way in which business matters are transacted by those who represent H.H. in Cairo. . . . Suppose a row was to take place and H.H. was rendered powerless (as so many princes have been of late years) where are we then and what guarantee is there that we should get a shilling of the money?"

In the summer of 1878 Ismail was often unwell himself. Three doctors attended him who, according to Mr. Bateman, were "determined to give him plenty of medicine. There is not one who knows what is the matter—one day he is treated with alkalis, then the three have a dispute and put him on acids—then another dispute and a change to mineral waters." The Englishman diagnosed the Khedive's illness as being caused by a mixture of very hot weather and worry.

Though on the whole the Khedive seems to have treated Mr. Bateman with kindness he sometimes received the rough edge of the royal tongue. "Unfortunately I fell into a little scrape the other day," he writes. "H.H. wanted an injection made—both the first and second attempts proved failures on account of the needle bending. I was present at the time so fortunately could explain the cause and calm down the anger. It was the Doctor's fault but, of course, I had to bear the blame. Two days after I was invited to breakfast with H.H. so imagine he has accepted my explanation. . . . You may feel sure that I shall leave nothing undone to get everything

settled, whatever may be the result of the constant pressure put on
H.H. by the consuls of the various European powers. England is
fast losing her power here. Why she should give way to France so
much I cannot imagine."

CHAPTER III

A MIND EXPANDS

W<small>HILE</small> Mr. Dispenser Bateman was penning the letter to Savory and Moore in which he mentioned the pressure that the European consuls were bringing to bear on Egyptian affairs, a young Egyptian of rare qualities was bending his full mind and energies to the problem of how to revive the spirit of his country, so that she could cure herself of the evils within her, in such fashion as would make European domination unnecessary.

He was a teacher of history at the time, and his name was Mohammed Abdu. He recognised the weak points of his nation which he felt were leading to Western domination, as inevitably as was Ismail's profligacy. He was willing to leave the latter problem to the experts, but with the points of character in the nation as a whole, he contended might and main.

His birth in an insignificant Egyptian village, in about 1847 was hailed by no one outside the village circle, for his father was a peasant in poor circumstances, though he eventually improved his lot by becoming a small land-owner. Mohammed Abdu's father was a man of character, and material advantages did not count overmuch in his scale of values, neither before nor after he had acquired them.

Life was no more easy for an Egyptian peasant in the eighteen fifties than it was in the eighteen seventies. Heavy taxation out of all proportion was extracted by the "bastinado" on the soles of the peasant's feet. Breadwinners were taken in chains as army recruits, to return years later, if at all, as physically broken men. From time to time minor officials descended on the villages, with whips, and drove all able-bodied men to work on clearing the canals, without pay and often without utensils. In that case the best that even a willing peasant could do was repeatedly to clap handfuls of mud on to the bare back of a companion, who would carry it thus from the canal bed to the ground level above.

So the boy, Mohammed Abdu, often listened to tales of oppression and wrong. They must have threaded through his mind and emotions as red wool in a weave. His father, who hated injustice, had stood up bravely to extortion with the result that in Mohammed

Abdu's infancy the family, persecuted by officials, had to flee from village to village.

Mohammed Abdu's father may have sensed something unusual in this, his youngest son, for he set his heart on giving him an education according to the country standards of the day which he had been unable to afford for his other children. Having learnt to read and write, Mohammed Abdu at the age of ten was sent to the home of a professional reciter of the Koran to learn the whole of the Holy Book by heart. This feat, phenomenal to European eyes, was the usual foundation of education for anyone of Mohammed Abdu's standing who wished to become a learned man. The very few schools run on European lines were only open to sons of officials. By the time he was twelve he had memorised the whole Koran. To have done this in two years was considered good progress. The whole village joined in the congratulations, and some parents hopefully removed their sons from a local Koran school to place them under Mohammed Abdu's tutor with a view to the same results from their own offspring.

The next stage of education now opened up for the lad. In 1862 he was sent to the school of the Ahmedi Mosque in Tanta. Here he learnt to recite and to intone the Koran, a more complicated task than it sounds, for details of emphasis and manner follow strict traditional rules. After two years of this he launched upon the choppy seas of Arabic grammar. His young and questing mind had so far weathered the frustrating experience of parrot-learning and of fettered imitation, but he was now set to memorise the whole text of an Arabic grammar and then the whole text of an incomprehensible commentary thereon, without a word of elucidation from his master.

For readers unacquainted with the nature of Arabic grammars it may be helpful to point out that they are not in the same category as the Victorian school grammar which opens with the sentence: "Little Emma came running into the room saying: 'Mamma, what is an adjective?'" Whereupon Mamma puts down her crochet and explains.

At the age of thirteen when his expanding mind was eager to understand the whys and wherefores, to judge for himself and to apply his learning, he was forced to spend hours conning such sentences as: "Speech consists of the orderly arrangement of sounds to impact meaning through position" and "inflection is the changing of the terminations of words in sound and function under the impact of various factors."

One day he decided that he really must try to elucidate some of these mysteries, so he arrived at class early to catch the attention of his master. "May I ask a question," he said, "what is the meaning of. . . ." Before he could finish his sentence the schoolmaster barked at him that no questions were allowed, and terminated the interview at once, with the Arabic equivalent of "Shut up and get out!" The boy was so dazed by this that he could do nothing but walk sadly back to his studies to cope in his despair as best he could.[1]

He struggled on till, quite suddenly, at the age of fifteen he felt he could stand it no longer. Mohammed Abdu rebelled. His frail ship of learning capsized entirely, and he swam gaily for the shores of freedom. His spirit revolted against schoolmasters whomsoever they might be and against book-learning in its entirety. He ran away to his maternal uncle's village where he was kindly received without bothersome questions. He spent three months riding and jousting with the other lads, before an older step-brother happened upon him and bore him protesting back to the Ahmedi Mosque. Up to it, but not into it. He absolutely refused to enter. He was so convinced that he would never succeed in studying and that his destiny was to till the fields as most of his family did, that he wore down his step-brother's efforts and returned to his home. His father was deeply disappointed but at first accepted the situation as it was; he also accepted Mohammed Abdu's intent to get married, which he did, at the age of 16, in 1865.

Forty days after the wedding, however, his father brought up the subject once more, and sternly this time, so Mohammed Abdu gave in and solemnly mounted the horse provided by his father to take him to the railway station en route to Tanta and that soul-destroying work. By his side was an escort detailed to see him safely into the train.

It happened to be blowing a "khamseen", the fierce hot wind of the spring, straight off the desert and laden with sand. Mohammed Abdu suggested that they waited in a village till it had died down. But his escort refused and tried to keep him going by force, as he had guessed, which was indeed the case, that Mohammed Abdu had hoped to elude him in the narrow village lanes. So it was now

[1] See *Mohammed Abduh* by Osman Amin, Cairo, 1944, p. 9.

or never for the boy. His horsemanship stood him in good stead and in an instant he was away, quicker than the howling wind, with the escort left so hopelessly behind that he gave up the chase.

The truant scholar made for another village where many of the inhabitants were related to his family.[2]

Here it was that fate caught up with him. All unwittingly foundations were laid for the plan of his life on a larger and nobler scale than anything aimed at by his father or evaded by himself.

The circumstances in which Mohammed Abdu sought asylum were soon the talk of the village. The following morning his great-uncle called on him—one Sheikh Darwish. It would be interesting to know the train of thought in the mind of the Sheikh, between hearing of Mohammed Abdu's precipitate arrival and calling to see him the next morning. It is not recorded but enough facts are known to deduce the thought behind them.

In the past Sheikh Darwish had travelled into the realm of Libya, as far as Tripoli. Here he had studied the Islamic learning and Sufi theology. He had then returned to Egypt, and seeking no spiritual laurels for himself, had tilled the fields as a working farmer. But what he had learnt of the ways of God with man did not remain pure theory. He knew that human nature could change and that it was meant to change. The presence of God in a man's heart, affecting character and conduct, was a reality to him. And he knew something of how that reality could be passed on to others. Mohammed Abdu himself related, at a later date, what took place among the green crops and humble mud-brick homes of that village.

Sheikh Darwish resolved to see his great-nephew as soon as the boy had had his first night's rest. The old man brought with him a manuscript treatise written by the hand of his own master in Libya. It dealt with the practical disciplines of the spiritual life.

He handed the book to the sullen lad. Mohammed Abdu refused it. "I wanted to look at it myself today", said his great-uncle, "but my eyes are too weak for reading."

He put the book gently into the boy's hands. It was thrown across the room. "God's curse on all books. I have no interest in reading now. God knows I hated it and all who make books their business."

The Sheikh asked, "My son, didn't you learn the Koran by heart?"

---

[2] For two varying versions of these events and the reasons for considering the above account authentic, see *Islam and Modernism in Egypt* by C. C. Adams, O.U.P., 1933, p. 25, n. 2.

"Yes, I know it. And I enjoyed reading and reciting it, but. . . ."
"But what?"
"The Agurrumiyah. That was the cause of my misery." (This
was a mediaeval treatise on classical Arabic grammar.)
"Never mind, don't fret yourself over it, my son. Why worry
about the Agurrumiyah? Look here. . . read a line and you will
see. . . ."

He still would not read, but the Sheikh, with patience and cour-
tesy, continued to question Mohammed Abdu and to draw forth
answers from his troubled soul. At last Mohammed Abdu consented
to read a few lines; and old Darwish explained what was read in a
simple, practical way.

After a short time, a group of young villagers called to the boy
to come and join them in their games. Throwing the book to one
side he ran out to play.

Sheikh Darwish was back with his book in the afternoon. Mohammed Abdu needed coaxing, but he read some more and the Sheikh
added his plain and patient comment on the subjects of the text.
The same thing happened the next day. As a grown man Mohammed
Abdu recorded that on the third day he had three hours of the book
without being for a moment tired or bored.

Sheikh Darwish was careful not to push home his triumph unduly.
He told the boy he had business to attend to and would have to
go now. This drew from Mohammed Abdu a request to borrow
the book, which was readily granted. He continued reading alone,
marking anything he did not understand, so as to remember to ask
his great-uncle about it when they met. Their conversations were
not now only about the book. Mohammed Abdu had really opened
his heart to the old man and learnt to love him.

The village lads now called to him in vain to come and join in
their sports. He had a thirst to be taught. He felt nourished by
the learning with which Sheikh Darwish could provide him. What
before stuck like a lump of dough was now digestible and satisfying.

After exactly a week of this the boy went a step further. He
began feeling his way from the intellectual to the spiritual which lay
behind it. He did not wait for the Sheikh to drop in on him, but
visited the old man in his home to ask him straight out what it was
that made him so different from most other men. "What is the way
you follow?" was his question. "Our way is the way of Islam", was
the answer. (The meaning of the word Islam is surrender to God.)

The boy had not expected this answer, knowing full well that everyone about him, men, women and children, called themselves Moslems, followers of Islam. "If they were Moslems," the Sheikh rejoined, "you would not see them squabbling over trifles or hear them invoking God while they utter falsehoods, which they do on the slightest pretext, and even without pretext."

These simple words burnt like fire in the boy's heart. He saw in a flash the difference between a label and the essence of the thing.

The Sheikh then advised him to go back to the Koran and read it in a new and living way. "How can I understand the Koran when I haven't learnt anything?" asked the boy—a strange question from one who could recite the book from the first chapter to the one hundred and fourteenth. "I shall read it with you. It will be enough if you understand it in a general way; by its very blessedness God will make the finer points clear to you. And when you are alone, call on God. . . ."[3]

Some eighteen hundred years before a rather similar conversation had taken place, not so far from where these two were talking. "And the angel of the Lord spake unto Philip, saying, Arise and go toward the south into the way that goeth down from Jerusalem unto Gaza, which is desert. And he arose and went: and, behold, a man of Ethiopia. . . was returning, and sitting in his chariot read Esaias the prophet. Then the Spirit said unto Philip, Go near, and join thyself to this chariot. And Philip ran thither to him, and heard him read the prophet Esaias, and said, Understandest thou what thou readest? And he said, How can I, except some man should guide me? And he desired Philip that he would come up and sit with him."[4]

Young Mohammed Abdu lost no time in practising what his great-uncle taught him, with the result that he soon found his outlook on life transformed. "But a few days had passed," he later wrote of himself, "when lo! you saw me soaring in spirit in a different world from that which I had known. The way which seemed to me straightened had widened out before me. The life of this world which had appeared great to me, had become small, and the acquirement of knowledge and the yearning of the soul towards

[3] For the words of these conversations see *Mohammed Abduh* by Dr. Osman Amin, translated by Charles Wendell, American Council of Learned Studies, Washington 1953, p. 66.
[4] *Acts of the Apostles*, Ch. 8, verses 26-31.

God which had been small in my eyes had become great; and all
my anxieties had been dispersed and there remained but one anxiety,
namely, that I should become perfect in knowledge, perfect in discipline of the soul."[5]

On the wings of this experience Mohammed Abdu returned
to Tanta, to the school of the Ahmedi Mosque, in October 1865.
How differently he now looked at it all! He listened anew, and
he understood. Old Sheikh Darwish had provided him with a key.
His fellow students soon noticed the change in him. They would
gather round to ask questions and to get his help with their work.

In a few months' time he felt a desire to join in the studies at the
great university mosque of Al Azhar. He felt that God was guiding
him to go there.

This most ancient foundation dates from the Fatimite dynasty
of Egypt and was first opened for worship in A.D. 971. Since then,
till the present day it has functioned as a centre for Islamic teaching.
It is certainly the oldest of its kind extant and in many ways is the
best known in the world.

From the tenth century till towards the end of the nineteenth,
the professors and teachers of Al Azhar received no salaries. Knowledge for its own sake was taken literally. Nor did the students
pay anything for the privilege of learning. Consequently life was
frugal for all concerned. Worthy men of the past had left endow-
ments to cover some of the expenses and also money to pay for
loaves of bread to be handed out free to both lecturers and students.
A student could enter the university when he felt competent to do
so and could sit at the feet of whatever professor he chose, and follow
whatever course of instruction he wished. He could continue to
learn till he felt he had acquired enough for his needs. If he wanted
to become, in his turn, a teacher at Al Azhar, and this wish was
approved by the senior members, he could take up his stand in a
corner of the great pillared court and hold forth on his subject.
The acid test was a simple one, whether he gathered students to
himself (who would sit cross-legged on the ground at his feet) and
having gathered them whether he retained their presence and their
attention, and for how long.

Students came then to Al Azhar, as indeed they come today, from
many distant lands. As you step over the threshold of the main
entrance, young men from Indonesia will be seen studying with

[5] See *Islam and Modernism in Egypt* by C. C. Adams, O.U.P., 1933, p. 24.

dark-skinned fellow Moslems from the Sudan or Abyssinia. North Africans and Chinese are there. Men from the Hedjas and paler faced men from Syria and the Lebanon walk softly, among Egyptians, Malayans and Turks. The arcades of the building are for prayer as well as study, so all comers remove their shoes according to Moslem custom. The total number of students in recent years has run into many thousands. For the year 1948, for instance, 18,582 pursued their studies at Al Azhar.

Though the look of the place has altered little in the last centuries, serious reforms started in 1872, with further reforms at intervals ever since. For what worked well in the middle ages proved most limiting in the nineteenth century. These reforms met with varying success. So time-honoured a place could always be relied on to produce a fierce reactionary group. For years Mohammed Abdu himself, when he was older, led the struggle of life against form, of living needs before dead letters. And a bitter struggle it proved to be.

But for the present, here he is, in the country train, having said goodbye to his wife and family, bound for Cairo and, for what seemed to him, the greatest seat of learning in the world. He would have been dressed as an Azhar student is dressed today. A soft red tarboush with a white muslin turban bound round it; a black kuftan, which is a form of long coat to the ankles worn over a white robe.

The country scenes, which he had loved so well, sped by. On either side of the railway lay some of the richest agricultural land in the world, the black Nile silt, chocolate-dark with goodness. Yet the peasant who worked it lived, for the greater part, in ignorance, illness and distress. Such contrasting thoughts might have been in Mohammed Abdu's mind, and he must have longed to bring to those people of his own blood his new-found liberation of spirit and of mind.

The beauty of that Delta landscape is no obvious beauty, but once sensed it can be most moving. A great hemisphere of sky is arched above it. The clover fields are brilliant green; the bearded wheat in spring is just merging from a pastel green into a pale hue like winter sunlight which in its turn becomes the deep amber yellow of early summer.

Each water wheel, turned by oxen or a great grey buffalo, emits a continuous sound, falling and rising, as the wheels turn round. It might be called a squeak by the unfeeling but to an Egyptian peasant it is melody, and the sound of his own water wheel spells all the love of home. It was February when Mohammed Abdu made this journey and the weeping willow trees which bend over the water courses would have their new green leaves breaking along each supple line of downward-falling strand, while, here and there, the first blossom of the apricots shows white, like porcelain against the winter branches, still dark without a leaf.

In February 1866, Mohammed Abdu had looked on such scenes for seventeen years, and loved them. By February 1866, my own father, Frederick Rowlatt, had completed his first year of life, spent also in Egypt, the first of very many, where he was soon to grow familiar with the same scenes and to know how they, and affection for the people for whom they formed the setting, could penetrate the soul. I too, fifty years later, was to know the same scenes and feel the same experience.

It was with eagerness that the young Mohammed Abdu started his studies at Al Azhar. He attended almost every lecture that could be fitted in to the twenty-four hours, as well as reading all he could lay hands on about the traditional subjects he was studying, such as grammar, jurisprudence and rhetoric. He always carried with him some book which he knew was interesting, and if the professor whose class he was attending proved to be dull or off the point, Mohammed Abdu would out with his book, and though still sitting with the group of students around the professor, he would read and cease to listen.

Mohammed Abdu would return to his own village for the summer recess, which, except for odd days here and there, was the only holiday of the year. Here he usually found that Sheikh Darwish had travelled from his own village to be close to his great-nephew during the summer. The old man would question him about the year's work. He would ask what he had learnt of logic, mathematics or geometry. To this the young man could only answer that some of these subjects were not even taught at Al Azhar. But Sheikh Darwish would not accept that as an excuse. He produced another of his simple sentences which left so deep an impression on his great-nephew. "The true student will not fail to find what he is looking for, no matter where he is."

So for the next few academic years Mohammed Abdu sought out the company of anyone who could broaden the basis of his education; sometimes he succeeded in getting help, but sometimes he failed.

During this time, as he was finding the intellectual nourishment he was offered increasingly arid and unprofitable, he concentrated more on what then seemed to him the right spiritual path to follow. He fasted often and prayed for long hours of the night. He shunned the company of human kind, more and more. He consciously cut down his conversation to the bare limits within which his mode of life could continue, and he tried various ascetic devices such as a rough garment next to his skin. With natural human contact thus cut off, he began to imagine that he could converse with the spirits of the dead.

When he arrived back to his home in this state, one summer, Sheikh Darwish felt the time had come again for some redirection. "I confessed to him," Mohammed Abdu says, "my disgust with the world, my horror at finding myself in the company of man, and my misery each time I found how far they were from the truth." To which the Sheikh replied, "But that is the principal reason for following the way I have shown you. For if all men were just and followed the way of truth, there would be no need for you."[6] If all was well with men, there would be no needs to fill. The thought lived in his mind that summer, as Sheikh Darwish pressed the point home. Knowledge was useless if it was no guiding light to himself or to others, argued the old man; Mohammed Abdu's knowledge would become a monopoly and a misfortune. The whole fulfilment of learning is to help guide others through the tangles of the world, was the tenor of his talk.

So the Sheikh, practical as ever, used to gather friends together after the day's work to discuss topics of interest. He would draw Mohammed Abdu into the talk in every possible way, and elicit his comments. Though reluctant and shy at first, the young man by degrees expressed himself more clearly and more often, till old Darwish was delighted to see an actual pleasure in the company gaining a stronger hold on Mohammed Abdu than had the previous melancholy withdrawal. When the time came to say good-bye again, the Sheikh wept as his great-nephew left for Cairo. In the following year the old man died.

The next months must have been perplexing ones for Mohammed Abdu. He knew that his great-uncle spoke with wisdom, and that he should be able to extract learning and inspiration in any circum-

[6] See Biographical Introduction to *Rissalat al Tawhid* by B. Michel and Sheikh Moustapha Abdul Raziq, Paris, 1925, p. xx.

stances. Yet he could not be blind to the fact that the spirit of expansion in mind and soul was almost entirely lacking in Al Azhar at that time. A minutiae of moribund technicalities overlaid the atmosphere; niceties of mediaeval grammar, unrelated to life, stifled original thought; frustration met him at every turn.

At this point in his life, a vital personality crossed his path, who was destined to wield great influence upon him. Sheikh Jamal al Din al Afghani was among the greatest Moslem teachers of the nineteenth century. His conception was to unite the Moslem world under one Islamic government and to restore the greatness and prestige of Islam to the same extent as it had existed in the days of the Caliphs of Damascus and Baghdad, or during the great Moslem Empire in Spain, or as the might of the Ayubite Dynasty when Saladin confronted the Crusaders with superior knowledge, higher culture and finally a greater force of power.

Jamal al Din, seeing into the future, felt called to warn all thinking Moslems that only by offensive action and drastic re-alignment of thought could the peoples of the Middle East avoid the domination of the West. This renaissance, he felt, could not be carried through without political revolution, and political revolution, given the circumstances of the day, might not succeed without political assassination. The flow of thoughts and of events might include the flow of blood. The man who expounded this call had a dynamo within him and a charm which greatly influenced his followers.

He paid a short visit to Egypt during which Mohammed Abdu called upon him, for his fame had gone before. Jamal al Din was at his evening meal where he was lodging in the Khan al Khalili,—the present bazaar, well-known to tourists, in the Musky quarter of Cairo. They were soon in deep conversation. The great Sheikh had an insight into man's mind possessed by all true teachers. His starting point was what Mohammed Abdu knew of, the orthodox interpretation of the Koran, and then the Sufi or mystical interpretation which had underlain the teachings of his great-uncle Sheikh Darwish. Jamal al Din knew he had met a young man of great latent powers, and Mohammed Abdu felt in the presence of someone who could help him cut the trammels of hidebound tradition and lead him on to that something for which he still searched.

Although Sheikh Jamal al Din soon left for Constantinople, in a year or two he was back in Cairo, for after an outspoken address in the former city he was expelled from it. Mohammed Abdu lost no time in seeking him out anew. He now studied with him regularly in the Sheikh's lodgings. Mohammed Abdu's enthusiasm drew other students to these gatherings. Their new teacher had a width of mind and liberality which made him welcome all comers equally, laying before them the fruits of his intellect and experience on many topics.

He led his pupils into the realms of history, philosophy, politics and sociology, and included many a European work translated into Arabic as a text book, which threw new light on much for these young men. Their teacher also trained them in public speaking and the art of expressing their thoughts in suitable form for the contemporary Arabic Press.

In all this Mohammed Abdu revelled and excelled. He contributed, among a number of other things, an article to the Egyptian newspaper, *Al Ahram*, then recently founded but today the oldest of the Cairo papers. This article dwelt on the glorious past of Egypt when she was reckoned to be among the greatest in the world, with a mature civilization when other lands had hardly emerged from barbarity. He then traced the moving of that civilization westwards, its development and growth, and went on to say how its attainments should now be welcomed back to Egypt to be fully used by her.

Jamal al Din continued, in the intellectual sphere, what Sheikh Darwish had begun in the simple human sphere of village life. He showed the young man how the doctrines of Sufism with their mystic and aesthetic trend, if over-emphasized, could lead to a retirement from the world of men and of strife which would accomplish nothing of change or of value. Jamal al Din argued thus from a background of Sufism in which he was as versed as was Mohammed Abdu, so his words carried weight, and the young man left his mystic visions behind him, though what was real in his religious experience was, if anything, enhanced.

As Mohammed Abdu's own output of writing increased he became well-known among his fellow students, who gathered round him, eager for the clarity of thought and expression which he had developed. He answered their questions and helped with their work. But he went further and began to give them instruction in philosophy and dogmatic theology. This also led him to work for hours in the Azhar library on books unconnected with the lectures being given by the professors at that time.

It is hardly to be wondered at that a deep-felt opposition was aroused among the university Sheikhs against both Jamal al Din and Mohammed Abdu, for their pride was hurt, and in varying degrees they were jealous. It must indeed have been irritating, especially as Mohammed Abdu did not keep quiet about it, but urged other scholars and would-be scholars to launch out into the wider application of learning and to use their own minds. Some of the attacks against Mohammed Abdu were not only on the grounds of dangerous modernism, contamination with Europe, and unorthodoxy but were spiteful and personal.

One day, it is reported, a small-minded and unsuccessful student made a point of slandering Mohammed Abdu to one of the Sheikhs who was particularly narrow in his outlook, by informing this Sheikh that Mohammed Abdu was spreading the Mu'tazilite teaching, which was known to be free-thinking.

He was soon summoned to the Sheikh to answer the charge. "I am informed you prefer the Mu'tazilite creed to that of al Ash'-ari"—a great defender of orthodoxy.

"If I have freed myself from Ash'arite traditionalism, how can mere adherence to the Mu'tazilite creed satisfy me? I am interested in finding proofs, not in chaining myself to any one form of received belief."

"Name someone who can bear you out in this."

"Who could possibly be a witness to such a thing? If there is one, let him come and distinguish between the two creeds; then let him tell us which one I prefer. Or perhaps someone like yourself who understands the Commentary? [On the creed of al Nasafi—a book which expresses some ideas in common with Mu'tazilite theories.] Here is the book and here am I. Question me if you will."[7] Nothing came of this conversation but further antagonism; Mohammed Abdu's replies had not been exactly oil on troubled waters.

In 1877 this antagonism took a decided form. By then Mohammed Abdu felt he had completed his studies at Al Azhar and wished to get the newly founded diploma and to take the necessary test. When he faced the board of examiners for the stiff oral examination, he found his particular opponent among the dignified Sheikhs lined up to question him.

Apparently, all save one had their sword into Mohammed Abdu, and had made up their minds to fail him, partly by a process of

[7] *Mohammed Abduh* by Osman Amin, translated by C. Wendell, op. cit., p. 19.

wearing him out, and partly by the most difficult and complicated questions they could concoct.

He managed so brilliantly, however, that the assembled Sheikhs were put to confusion and started arguing among themselves. Sheikh al Abbasi, Mohammed Abdu's one friend, spoke up well for him, saying that as there was nothing higher than a first class diploma, a first class was what he should get. Though greatly outnumbered he stuck to his point, and eventually a compromise was reached and Mohammed Abdu was grudgingly awarded a second class diploma.

Quite undeterred by this rebuff, Mohammed Abdu flung himself into his task of teaching in the new spirit which he felt himself called to spread. He chose new subjects, new textbooks and new methods as vehicles for spreading his ideas of how young Egypt of his day could best serve its religion, its country and its down-trodden compatriots. A main emphasis of his theme was how they could change events themselves, before the crumbling edifice around them reached the point when it would be impossible to keep out foreign intervention.

When he was not lecturing in Al Azhar he was lecturing in his own home. His enthusiasm was catching, and he was always the centre of an eager crowd of students. He lectured on ethics, which was considered most unusual. He used Guizot's *History of Civilisation in Europe and in France* which had recently been translated into Arabic.

It appears that at about this time Mohammed Abdu joined the Egyptian branch of the Masonic Order, which was affiliated to the Order in England. He hoped thereby to widen his sphere of ideas.

In 1878 he was appointed teacher of history at the Dar al Ulum. This was a college founded a few years previously in an endeavour to train the traditional type of Al Azhar teacher in some modern methods and modern subjects.

Here his course of lectures was based on the Prolegomena of Ibn Khaldun, the great Arab philosophical historian of the fourteenth and fifteenth centuries. He used this historian's ideas on why nations rose and fell, what constituted civilization and the principles of human society, as a basis for his own thoughts and vision for his country, applying them practically to conditions of the day.

Another medium through which he worked was the Arabic language and its literature of which he was appointed teacher in the Khedival School of Languages. Here he set to work vigorously to rectify some of the methods under which he had suffered as a child in the Ahmedi Mosque at Tanta.

CHAPTER IV

AN ABDICATION, A PAPER, AND A CAUSE

WHILE Mohammed Abdu was working at full stretch to alter his country's fate by dealing with what seemed to him fundamentals, the actual political scene was developing feverishly. He eagerly grasped at the independent thought and full liberty of reason which he deemed to be the fruits of Western mental attitudes, but in other respects he wished to keep the West at arm's length. What was actually happening around him, however, was an inundation of Western influence based almost entirely on materialism at its most florid. This civilization which Ismail was helping to usher in, was the very sort to lead, with ever increasing pace, to that foreign domination against which Mohammed Abdu sought to fortify his religion and his land.

The misrule in Egypt, while being in part fanned by Europeans, was naturally viewed most gravely by official Europe. The Egyptian debts were affecting international finance, and something had to be done about it. In 1876 Ismail had accepted the Commission of the Debt and in 1878 he reluctantly employed two European ministers, a Frenchman and an Englishman (Mr. Rivers Wilson)[1] to advise him on important matters. It was not long, however, before he dismissed them both.

There was a general feeling among the Great Powers that Ismail himself was the real cause of the trouble and that he must change his ways or go. It remained for France and Britain to take action.

After discussion with Paris, Lord Salisbury sent the following despatch to Great Britain's representative in Egypt: "The Khedive is well aware that the considerations which compel Her Majesty's Government to take an interest in the destinies of Egypt have led them to pursue no other policy than that of developing the resources and securing the good government of the country. They have hitherto considered the independence of the Khedive and the maintenance of his dynasty as important conditions for the attainment of these ends; and the same sentiments have, they are well assured, animated the Government of France. . . . We prefer to look to his [Ismail's] future action for a favourable interpretation

[1] He was knighted in 1880.

28

of the conduct he has lately pursued. But if he continues to ignore the obligations imposed upon him by his past acts and assurances and persists in declining the assistance of European Ministers whom the two powers may place at his disposal, we must conclude that the disregard of engagements which has marked his recent action was the result of a settled plan, and that he deliberately renounces all pretension to their friendship. In such a case, it will only remain for the two Cabinets to reserve to themselves an entire liberty of appreciation and action in defending their interests in Egypt, and in seeking the arrangements most calculated to secure the good government and prosperity of the country."

The French and British Consuls-General laid these views before the Khedive, who felt himself unable to accept them. Two months later, in June 1879, the next move was taken. The Khedive received the following: "The French and English Governments are agreed to advise Your Highness officially to abdicate and to leave Egypt. Should Your Highness follow this advice, our Governments will act in concert in order that a suitable Civil List should be assigned to you and that the order of succession in virtue of which Prince Tewfik [Ismail's son] will succeed Your Highness should not be disturbed. We must not conceal from Your Highness that if you refuse to abdicate, and if you compel the Cabinets of London and Paris to address themselves directly to the Sultan, you will not be able to count either upon obtaining the Civil List or upon the maintenance of the succession in favour of Prince Tewfik."

Ismail's first reaction on receiving the ultimatum was to ask for time and then to get in touch with the Sultan in Constantinople. There seemed a chance that the Sultan might support his vassal against the European Powers; but for once Europe was united. The Ambassadors were instructed to show plainly to the Sultan how ill-advised he would be to prevent the plan of Ismail's forced abdication.

Consequently the required telegram was sent indicating that His Imperial Majesty the Sultan invited the Khedive Ismail to relinquish his post. To make the point clear it was addressed "to the ex-Khedive Ismail", while a simultaneous telegram was sent to his son Tewfik nominating him and addressing him as Khedive.

The King of Italy offered Ismail a villa at Naples for his retirement. So the royal yacht Mahroussa steamed out of Alexandria harbour for Italy in the June sunshine of 1879, just as in 1952 the royal yacht

Mahroussa steamed in the same direciton carrying Ismail's grandson, ex-King Farouk, away from Egypt, presumably for ever. Both left with dignity. And on both occasion those gathered to say good-bye found it hard to hide their emotion. But it should be remembered that both rulers were fundamentally foreigners in Egypt. Different blood flowed in their veins and different thoughts moulded their minds, from the blood and the thoughts which made up the Egyptian nationalist of the nineteenth century and again of the twentieth century.

In 1879 my grandfather, J. E. Cornish, was back in Egypt, in charge of the Alexandria Waterworks, and some weeks before the abdication he was received by Ismail for the last time. "The interview was a very stormy one," he recalled. "Even in those days Ismail was not a pleasant man to face in his wrath, and I well remember shaking myself with a feeling of relief when I got outside the Abdin Palace that day, although I was not the immediate object of his anger, which was raised by a telegram he had received in my presence from the President of the Court of Appeal in Alexandria, flatly refusing to obey his order to register a contract until the fees had been paid in cash by the Egyptian Government. The amount was sufficiently large to make it very inconvenient just at that time to find the money; and it was my uncomfortable duty to tell the Khedive, that until the contract was duly registered, I was unable to comply with a wish he had strongly expressed.

"Although for some time past the Khedive Ismail had been seeing the shady side of things, I doubt if any one in this country had dared to oppose him so openly, and he seemed to resent it most bitterly. In all my previous communications with him, which had now lasted over eight years, I had always been treated by him with greater consideration than a man in my position was likely to expect. I regretted this change in the last interview I was ever to have with him. When, a short time after, I saw him going on board his yacht at Alexandria, a broken down man, leaving his own country without hope of return, it was a sad contrast with the man as I had known him only a short time before, holding in his grasp influence and wealth beyond the dream of avarice."

Before the fall of the Khedive Ismail, the Sheikh Jamal al Din al Afghani and his followers had sought out Prince Tewfik and informed him of their hopes for reform, and above all of their strong opinion that some form of national assembly should be constituted **through** which the people of Egypt could have a voice in the affairs of state.

It is said that Tewfik not only listened attentively but promised his support when the time came for him to wield the power which was then his father's. On the strength of this, Jamal al Din, Mohammed Abdu and others of their liberal-thinking group felt that a new era might well be on the way. The royal Mahroussa with her golden painted prow steaming towards Europe represented more to them than a change of ruler. In Tewfik they had hopes.

So it was a rude shock when, in the middle of a night in September 1879, Sheikh Jamal al Din al Afghani was woken by loud knocks on his door, was bundled into a sealed carriage and from there put on a train for Suez, under escort. Expelled from Egypt, he sailed to India, where he lived for some years. On Mohammed Abdu fell as surprising a blow though a lighter one. He was relieved of his duties in the Dar al Ulum and the School of Languages. He was told to go to his village and stay there, and from there to make no touch with the Egyptian public—neither by written article nor by speech. This was done at the Khedive's instigation, or at least by his consent.

There is but little evidence to show what lay behind Tewfik's change of attitude. Sheikh Rashid Rida, the chief Arabic biographer of Mohammed Abdu, says that Jamal al Din had lost no time in visiting the new Khedive, reminding him of his promises, and pressing most forcefully for the convocation of a national assembly. It is easy to picture the bearded, turbanned elder expounding his convictions to the young Khedive sitting nervously among the Louis Philippe furniture of his ornate palace, in his dark Stambouli coat buttoned to the neck. He would have seen the fire in Sheikh Jamal al Din's eyes and felt the furnace of his breath. "Where might this all end?" he could have thought. With the reins of government so newly in his hands, he may well have decided, there and then, that as it was in his power to get rid of the Sheikh, he would indeed get rid of the Sheikh.

Other writers (among them Professor Edward Browne) suggest that Tewfik acted on the advice of Englishmen in Egypt whose influence was rapidly mounting. This could have been either because Tewfik was convinced that they were right or that he was unable to stand against their opinion. And as for Mohammed Abdu, the Khedive would have had backing enough from the old Sheikhs of Al Azhar, to give the order of banishment from public life.

Professor Browne reported that Sheikh Jamal al Din al Afghani's last words on Egyptian soil, were: "I leave you Sheikh Mohammed Abdu; he is sufficient for Egypt."[2]

At the time that action was taken against these two Sheikhs, the Prime Minister of Egypt, Riyad Pasha, was out of the country. On his return, he was shocked to hear of Mohammed Abdu's punishment. In his opinion it was unfair. He lost no time in getting him granted a pardon. He went further and appointed Mohammed Abdu as one of the three editors of the official organ of the government, called *Egyptian Events*. This was a publication made up almost entirely of official announcements from the various government departments, with a few descriptions of local events added thereto. As a vehicle of thought and influence it was neither popular nor inspiring; but with characteristic vigour Mohammed Abdu set about changing it, for he felt himself called to use any medium that came his way for the furthering of his ideas. If he found himself third editor of one of the dullest and dimmest of government publications that it was possible to imagine, this was to him a God-sent opportunity of transforming the situation.

One of the first things he did was to draw up a programme of proposed reforms for enlarging the scope and quality of the paper. This was submitted to the Prime Minister and approved by a committee. On the strength of it, Mohammed Abdu found himself chief editor with the power to employ assistants of the calibre he needed. It is noteworthy that one of these men on whom he picked was Sa'ad Zaghlul, then a student at Al Azhar, aged twenty one, the same Sa'ad Zaghlul who was to have such bitter duels with successive British Governments in the nineteen-twenties.

An aspect of *Egyptian Events* which called for immediate reform was the fact that it was distributed among officials and heads of villages, whether they desired it or whether they did not. This distribution had, of course, to be followed by the still more unpopular move of gathering in payment for it. The unwilling recipient had "to pay its rates by the same means as was used to compel property owners to pay theirs",[3] remarked Mohammed Abdu laconically, knowing only too well what those means could be.

To help win voluntary readers the new editor made it a rule that Government departments and the courts of law were to produce

[2] *The Persian Revolution* by E. G. Browne, Cambridge, 1910, p. 74.
[3] *Mohammed Abduh*, Osman Amin, translated by Charles Wendell, p. 26.

for publication, not only what actions and decisions they had already taken, but what they were in process of deciding and what they were considering as possibilities for the future. This may not sound a dramatic step towards enlarging circulation—no free trips to Russia or America were offered, no gifts of detergents to be delivered weekly for life came the way of readers of *Egyptian Events*—but the simple fact of getting the government to put its cards on the table began to win the confidence of the public in the official journal.

The next point to feel the full impact of Mohammed Abdu's zeal was the actual literary standard of the work. If this did not come up to the expected level, those who were responsible for the contributions were asked to attend night schools which were specially opened for the purpose. In some of these, the "pupils" were a little astonished to find their instructor was Mohammed Abdu himself. His chief aim was to show how the old long-winded phraseology so wrapped up the meaning it meant to convey that the unravelling of it was a work of patience and love unlikely to be undertaken by a subscriber whose payment for the journal had been wrung from him by a beating on the soles of his feet.

As editor-in-chief of *Egyptian Events*, Mohammed Abdu was also director of the Department of Publications, which post then carried with it the right of censorship over all newspapers printed in Egypt, including foreign ones. If a paper brought charges against any government official, those charges were to be investigated by the Government, and if no evidence could be found the paper was warned, for its first offence, then suspended for further offences, or even suppressed for doing so too often.

He also spread his forceful call for a better use of the Arabic language beyond the limits of his own paper. One leading journal was informed that its publication might well be suspended if it did not find itself an editor with literary ability by a specified date. These rather drastic methods certainly brought results. Men with real gifts found their way to the top and government departments became competitive in putting their points with clarity.

In spite of *Egyptian Events* being a government organ, Mohammed Abdu was very outspoken in his criticisms of some government officials through the medium of his own editorials. A certain governor of Beni Suef came in for adverse comment. In great rage he banned the paper from his province, and appealed to the Minister of Interior saying that all stable government was undercut if he, the Governor, was criticised. But his protest gathered no backing.

The same thing happened in the Department of Education. Not only were abuses uncovered here but practical measures of reform were suggested. The Head of the Department being unused to such treatment protested vehemently, but was told that if any of the charges proved to be false the official journal would publish the fact. The challenge was not accepted. Some of Mohammed's own contributions to *Egyptian Events* show clearly his philosophy of evolutionary change for his nation. "It is not only an error," he wrote, "it is the essence of ignorance itself, to burden the people with a way of life of which they can have no true conception. . . . It is just as pointless as to demand of an individual, things with which he has no connection and which he does not even know how to attain. It is only the part of wisdom to retain their customs when they are universally ingrained in the minds of every one of them. Then let a few improvements, not too far removed from their current level, be introduced. And when they have grown accustomed to them, let others be attempted on a higher plane. . . .

"But. . .if demands they are incapable of fulfilling are made, and they are given the power, without the habit of ruling, I can see them floundering along a road whose end is not in sight, confused and misled by ideas foreign to them."[4]

Mohammed Abdu's character of teacher and reformer had by now overlaid the philosophy of violent revolution taught him by Jamal al Din, yet he was still feeling out for the ideal form of government for Egypt of the day. His mind turned to the possibilities of dictatorship, which he expressed in an article called, "Should a Benevolent Despot Rise in the East?" The idea that human nature should change is inherent in this article but the true secret of how it should be done evades him. Some of it reads almost as if his patience and forbearance with mankind were running low. Had his greatuncle Darwish dealt with him, when he was a puzzled, obstinate run-away schoolboy, as he suggests the despot might deal with people, he, Mohammed Abdu, would surely not have changed in the way he did.

Yet the very words, mistaken in philosophy though some of them may be, are filled with a yearning to bring change to his people. "He is a despot who forces those who pretend not to know one

[4] *Mohammed Abduh* by Osman Amin, translated by C. Wendell, op. cit., p. 29.

another, to acknowledge one another's existence. He compels people to behave with forbearance towards one another and constrains neighbours to deal justly with one another. He brings people around to his opinion of what is good for them through fear, if they do not voluntarily take the trouble to find the means to their own happiness.

"The just despot will take no step without thinking first of the people he rules, and if any personal happiness should offer itself to him, it will always be a secondary consideration, for he belongs to them more than to himself. In fifteen years he will bow the necks of the powerful for their own good as well as for their descendants. He will treat the disease of character to which they are subject with the most efficacious remedies—among them amputation and cauterisation, if the condition warrants it. Within this space of time he will form the minds of the masses in accordance with the ends he has in view, and will channelize their ambitions through education, taking as good care of them as the planter of his tree. . . in fifteen years he will muster up a great multitude who will support reform. . . .

"The first step towards a certain measure of freedom being the formation of municipal councils. After a number of years provincial councils would follow, provided that they be not instruments that are swayed this way and that, but sources of ideas and opinions. After that will follow representational parliaments."[5]

Some of Mohammed Abdu's ideas on the place of a creed in people's lives are interesting. "Every man who holds to his religion, be he Moslem, Christian or Jew, should not send his children, while they are small and only see through the eyes of the master and educators, to a school where the teaching and direction are in the hands of people who do not belong to their [the children's] religion. . . . But he who has a personal conception of religion, and who belongs to no actual church, can send his children to any school, and at any age. . . . Above all, we wish to draw the attention of fathers of families (may God guide them), not to give their children an education which ends in troubling their spirit and creating disorder in their thoughts."[6]

As Mohammed Abdu continued to express his conviction that

[5] *Mohammed Abduh* by Osman Amin, translated by C. Wendell, op. cit., p. 34.
[6] *Rissalat al Tawhid*, translated by B. Michel and Sheikh Moustapha Abdu Raziq, Paris, 1925, p. xxxii.

Egypt's need was for internal reform to be achieved by her own efforts, the chief Egyptian actor in the coming drama was moving to the centre of the stage.

He was Ahmed Arabi, a soldier whose ideas were often vague and fraught with feeling rather than tempered by thought. He was deeply conscious, however, of being an Egyptian in company with millions of other Egyptian peasants and workers, living their lives subservient to a ruling dynasty and ruling class of foreign origin and ways. His deep desire was somehow to alter this situation.

As was the case with Mohammed Abdu, he came on to the stage from the wings of obscurity. Ahmed Arabi was born in an Egyptian Delta village near Zagazig some nine or ten years before Mohammed Abdu saw the light of day. His father was of rather more substance than was Mohammed Abdu's, but in character he was probably less outstanding. He was Sheikh of the village and owned eight and a half acres of land. Young Ahmed was sent to the village school where he learnt his letters and memorised passages of the Koran. His father had done a short course of study at Al Azhar before returning to till his acres, and he was keen that his son Ahmed should do the same. So the lad was sent to Cairo at the age of twelve and drank what he could from the fountain of learning for two years. He was a tall, well-built boy, so when the recruiting officers visited his neighbourhood, he was taken, there and then, for the army. Nor could his sorrowing family raise enough money to buy him off.

Said Pasha, who was ruler of Egypt before Ismail (after whom Port Said was named), made a point of encouraging young men of local Egyptian race. Any likely looking son of a Sheikh was noted for special training in the army. Young Arabi was given a form of examination and was then made an army clerk, at 60 piastres a month (about 12/-). However, this line did not take his fancy, for he himself admitted that he was ambitious at that age and wished to become a personage like the Governor of his province. This individual, whoever he was, had obviously impressed Ahmed as a small boy, and fourteen was still not far removed from being a small boy.

So he asked the man under whom he served if he could be put in the ranks, with a view to working his way up. Nor was he diverted from his purpose when it was made clear to him that under those circumstances his pay would be only 50 piastres a month. He did ell and was soon put through some other examination and was promoted—then another which made him a lieutenant when only seventeen.

A remarkable character, Suliman Pasha al Fransawi, took notice of this young man whose promotion he accelerated till he found himself a Colonel at the age of twenty-two. This astronomical rise was told by Ahmed Arabi, years later, when as an old man he was recounting the story of his life. So whether the Ruritanian rapidity of his rise was quite accurate, or whether viewed from a distance it became speeded up, is uncertain.

Suliman Pasha al Fransawi, i.e. the Frenchman, had been a Colonel Sèves formerly of the French army, who had settled in Egypt, served in the Egyptian army, become a Moslem and married a member of the ruling family. He was, in fact, a forbear of Queen Nazli, ex-King Farouk's mother. All visitors to modern Cairo are familiar with his statue in Suliman Pasha Square. In 1862 Said Pasha went on a journey to Medina, the burial place of the Prophet Mohammed. As one of his A.D.C.'s he took with him young Ahmed Arabi. One day during the journey, Said Pasha was reading an Arabic translation of the life of Napoleon. As he read the chapter dealing with Napoleon's conquest of Egypt, he became so angry that he threw the book on the ground at Arabi's feet, saying: "See how your countrymen let themselves be beaten." Even Said Pasha, who partially considered himself Egyptian, which some of his successors did not begin to do, when talking to Arabi, said "your countrymen" rather than "our countrymen".

Arabi picked up the book and took it away with him. He read it through the night. Next morning he told Said Pasha that the French had won the Battle of the Pyramids because they were better drilled and organised, but that "we could do as well in Egypt if we tried".

In spite of Said Pasha's patronage of Arabi, there came a time when he dismissed him. It was because Arabi had objected to an order of Said Pasha's, liberating soldiers from observing the Ramadan fast. Arabi thought this was wrong and he said so.

In 1863 Said Pasha died and Ismail took his place. The new ruler held no brief for officers of Egyptian blood, thinking it more sensible in every way to promote those of his own race—the Turks and Circassians. So now Arabi's rising star began to set, he was only given routine transport jobs or at best a few dull undertakings which could have been done by a civilian. He was not alone singled out for such treatment. It came the way of his fellow Egyptian officers too. They became men with a grievance.

There may have been an understandable element of pique in Arabi's reactions, but the main trends of his thoughts and words were the championing of a cause—the cause of the men of his own blood and bone who were being unjustly treated. This appeared to motivate him more deeply than frustrated ambition. He also developed a power of expressing himself in a way which appealed to his countrymen, including the most humble. His few years at Al Azhar and his own personal faith in God helped him to illustrate his thoughts with quotations from the Koran, whose fine rolling periods, well declaimed, have ever stirred the emotions of an Arab audience.

In 1872 Ismail sent an Egyptian army into the north Abyssinian province of Bogos and captured it. Some time later this army of occupation was routed by the Abyssinians. The following year another Egyptian army attacked Abyssinia and was again defeated. In the first instance the Egyptian army was commanded by a Swiss, and in the second by a Dane.

Two years later Ismail launched a third and larger force led by Ratib Pasha, of Circassian extraction. But Ratib was especially told by Ismail himself, to leave the actual conduct of battle to an American, General Loring, who was accompanied by other American officers. All the minor sections were commanded by Circassians. Personal feelings, rivalries and disputes reigned supreme, and it is hardly to be wondered at that the Egyptian army again suffered a disastrous defeat.

Ahmed Arabi was given a job in charge of transport during this campaign. In recounting later his disgust at the situation he mentioned the presence of another strange individual, a French priest who according to Arabi visited General Loring daily, advising him in detail on what his next moves should be. This Machiavellian cleric, it seems, then passed on all the news to the Abyssinian King Yohannes. The next thing the Egyptian army knew was the advance of an Abyssinian multitude of 300,000 soldiers, women and old men (!) it is recorded, which, in spite of the inclusion of the last two categories (or possibly because of them), overwhelmed the Egyptians.

It was called the Egyptian army, but apart from the underfed and underpaid rank and file and a few officers given negligible responsibility, it was not Egyptian in the true sense of the word. Ismail considered arraigning the commanding officers before a council of war on their return, but, says Arabi, he gave up this idea when one of the Circassians turned out to be a man who had already attempted to murder some ministers at Constantinople, Ismail presumably thought that this man might employ such tactics again, this time nearer home, if provoked. The American officers, however, were dismissed, and were only paid their indemnities after the United States Consul had held lengthy and persistent negotiations with Ismail on the subject.

Arabi himself had a charge of corruption brought against him and was moved aside in disgrace. Mr. Moberly Bell, for many years *The Times* Correspondent in Egypt before he became manager of *The Times*, comments thus on the incident: "I may as well at once say that a charge so frequently and unjustly made against any man whom it is desirable to get rid of, does not really discredit the accused. From what I can learn, it is far more probable that Arabi showed some insubordination, or possibly opposed peculation in his superiors, than that he himself was guilty of it. The charge proves nothing more than that someone wanted to get rid of him."[7]

So while Mohammed Abdu was struggling to free himself from the dead trammels of Islamic tradition at Al Azhar and clashing head on with its exponents, Ahmed Arabi was feeling in his mind and in his hurt emotions the injustice of authority as exemplified in Egypt of his day. There had earlier been a small incident which had turned him personally against Ismail in particular. Soon after Said Pasha's death Arabi had been on guard at the Palace, and Ismail had issued an order that he was to be punished and removed for making too much noise outside the Palace windows— for being noisier than the big drum and of less use, was the simile used.

During his enforced leisure after the Abyssinian campaign, Arabi attended lectures at Al Azhar and here he was aware of Mohammed Abdu's presence though he does not seem to have met him.

After some months, Arabi was again employed by the army.

[7] *Khedives and Pashas* by One Who Knows Them Well. Sampson Low, 1884, p. 60. This work, for some time anonymous, is now attributed to Mr. Moberley Bell.

This time he began to take seriously his connection with a secret society of Egyptian officers that had existed for some time, the chief purpose of which was to end the favouritism shown to Circassians and to depose Ismail. Discontent was rife in the army, for salaries had not been paid for months, when a new ministry under Nubar Pasha, an Armenian, decided to place a large number of officers on the half-pay list. "This measure would, under any circumstance, have been considered harsh, however necessary it might have been in view of the straitened condition of the Egyptian Treasury," commented Lord Cromer in his book, *Modern Egypt*. "It was, however, especially harsh and impolitic to dismiss so large a body of officers without, in the first place, fully liquidating the arrears of pay due to them. The result was that many officers and their families were reduced to a state of complete destitution."[8]

The discontent was bound to show itself in some form sooner or later—it happened to be sooner. On 18 February 1879, Nubar Pasha and Mr. Rivers Wilson (the English Minister whom Ismail was shortly to dismiss unceremoniously) were driving to their offices when their carriages were surrounded by an angry gang of officers armed with swords. They were roughly treated, moustache-pulling and ear-boxing being considered suitable indignities, and bustled into the nearby Ministry of Finance where they were locked in and the telegraph wires were cut.

The news penetrated to Lord Vivian, the British Consul-General, who went straight to the Khedive Ismail. Together they drove to the Ministry of Finance. The large crowd round the building gave way on seeing the Khedive in person. Demanding to see the prisoners, Vivian and the Khedive were shown to an upper room full of soldiers standing guard over the two distinguished men, who were not seriously hurt.

The Khedive ordered the officers to leave at once, and told them that their grievances would be looked into later. "If you are my officers," he boomed, "you are bound by your oath to obey me; if you refuse I will have you swept away." Lord Vivian reported: "They obeyed him although reluctantly and with some murmuring, begging him to leave them to settle their accounts in their own way."

It so happened that my grandfather, J. E. Cornish, accompanied a friend who had an appointment with Mr. Rivers Wilson at the Ministry of Finance, on that same day. "When we got near the

[8] *Modern Egypt* by Lord Cromer, Macmillan, 1911, p. 57.

Ministry we were stopped by soldiers," he said. "I thought they were possibly Ismail's body-guard, and explained to an officer that we came by appointment. I could get no answer except that they had orders to let no one pass. With the exception of being inflexible, the soldiers appeared to be quiet and orderly, and I doubt if most of them had any more idea than we had as to what they were there for."

My grandfather here interpolated a comment on the sort of people likely to be met with in the ante-room of the Ministry of Finance in those days. "I saw a lady who was one of the recognised leaders of Cairo society, she told us that she had come to borrow from the Minister some of the pretty things around, such as mirrors, curtains and candelabra for the decoration of her residence, on the occasion of a ball, to which she invited us, as a set-off for waiting while she interviewed the Minister.

"The Ministry of Finance was at that time just as it was taken over from being the harem of the ill-fated Minister of Finance who had been murdered at Ismail's command. The walls were decorated in the most florid style by Parisian artists, the panels were filled with gods and goddesses of the gayest type. I had watched Ismail on more than one occasion sitting in this place and amid these surroundings and wondered if his thoughts ever reverted or his conscience ever troubled him as to the former owner," continued my grandfather.

(I myself, well remember, as a child, hearing my parents talk of the old Chief of Police, of whom it was impolitic to ask what accident had caused the loss of his thumb. For it was supposed to have been he who had been ordered by Ismail to kill the former owners of this mansion; and his thumb had been bitten off in the struggle.)

But to return to Ahmed Arabi. He was not among the disbanded soldiers and had nothing to do with the rough handling of Nubar and Rivers Wilson. He was able to prove that he had been in Rosetta till the night before. But none the less he was arrested and punished by being separated from his regiment. The board, before whom he had to appear, included an American, General Stone, who was at that time serving in Ismail's army. Arabi was sent to Alexandria in disgrace and given the job of agent for some Upper Egypt Sheikhs whose arrears of taxes had been collected in beans and other crops and transported to Alexandria as security for the money which certain Jews of Alexandria had advanced to Ismail.

Two other officers who were questioned with Arabi were also ordered away to obscure posts. Arabi's own words, as in age he recollected the time, read with a great simplicity and an unconscious prophecy: "Before we separated we had a meeting at which I proposed that we should join together and depose Ismail. It would have been the best solution of the case, as the Consuls would have been glad to get rid of Ismail in any way, and it would have saved after complications as well as the fifteen millions Ismail took away with him when he was deposed. [The deposition happened shortly after the meeting with his brother officers, of which Arabi speaks.] But there was nobody as yet to take the lead, and my proposal though approved was not executed. The deposition of Ismail lifted a heavy load from our shoulders and all the world rejoiced, but it would have been better if we had done it ourselves as we could then have got rid of the whole family of Mohammed Ali, who were none of them, except Said, fit to rule and we could have proclaimed a republic."[9] Seventy-three years later Egyptians were able to fulfil this wish.

[9] *Secret History of the English Occupation of Egypt* by W. S. Blunt, Fisher Unwin, 1907, p. 483.

PART II

THE DRAMA IS PLAYED—1882

CHAPTER V

THE ARMY ACTS

DURING the summer of 1879 grave misgivings were felt by sections of the English public about the complicated footholds England was laboriously making for herself in Egypt.

The Times editorial of 1 August 1879, took the line that, although Ismail's departure and Tewfik's enthronement were regarded as triumphs of European diplomacy, yet the advantages gained by the interference it had necessitated, did not justify the risks inherent in such a policy. The price of possible financial stability might well prove too high. It was not as if England was in the vigorous days of Lord Palmerston, argued the editorial, when she could freely indulge in independent action of the type expressed by Lord Palmerston himself when he stated that, if difficulties arose with Egypt, Mohammed Ali would be "chucked into the Nile".

Even in 1877, the editorial recollected, the British Government had deemed fit to bring Indian troops to the Mediterranean and naturally no complaints had been heard from the Egyptian Government. But Egypt had now become a type of joint stock concern with France, Germany, Austria, Italy and Russia as England's partners. If some similar contingency arose, the Powers, as Board of Directors of Egyptian affairs, might object to England's ideas. Russia in particular, it was noted, would be sure to interpose a veto and insist on pushing the doctrine of Egyptian neutrality to its ultimate consequences. Such were the future difficulties, that the British Government must be prepared to meet, as foreseen by *The Times*.

It is plain from a study of this lengthy editorial that many Englishmen were afraid that the interference of the British Government in Egyptian affairs might have awkward consequences in connection with Turkey. The effect of the new policy on Egyptians themselves was not thought to be worth much consideration, as no tangible body representing Egypt herself was deemed to exist. In the meantime, however, something was fast forming which called itself the Egyptian Nationalist Party. It was formed on the basis of the officers' secret society which was widened to include other non-military personalities. The scene of their meetings and discussions was Hel-

45

wan, a small town south of Cairo. Arabi was among the leaders.

On 4 November 1879, a manifesto was issued as from the Egyptian National Party. Mr. M. Sabry, the Egyptian historian, says that as far as he could trace, only one copy of the whole text still exists; it is in French, in the Bibliothéque Nationale de Paris.[1] It is a most interesting document to read today and to compare with the variously expressed aims of the Egyptian revolution of 1952.

Whatever one may think of this 1879 expression of nationalism it was certainly a cry from the heart, a cry which in different styles has been repeated for nearly eighty years and in Egyptian eyes has only now been answered. If the eventual fulfilling of these fundamental national desires has been achieved with some explosions, it is hardly surprising.

Any observer of the present Egyptian scene is free to form his opinion of it, but when past facts are known there is surely no place for self-righteous astonishment. Any observation beginning with the words "How can. . .?" must be suspect from whatever quarter it comes, whether it is "How can the Egyptians be so ungrateful?" or "How can the English be so obdurate?" First seek out an answer to the "How can?" question, with diligence and an open mind, not leaving it as a rhetorical question needing no answer save an outraged surprise. Then in the light of what answer emerges judgements can be formed. Given sincerity, constructive thought can begin.

"Must Egypt be nothing but a geographical expression?" wrote Arabi and his friends in this 1879 manifesto. "Must her 5 million inhabitants [there are now 23 million] be as cattle over which are imposed drovers at will. . .?" What they ask is to be treated as their brothers in Europe would wish to be treated if placed in the same position as Egyptians are placed."

The authors of this document go on to state that they wish to save Egypt from the abyss into which arbitrary rule and usury had plunged her and that they view this as a sacred duty and indisputable right. The Egyptian people are now emancipated, they say, and wish for no more slavery. One of their expressed aims was to raise the level of the Egyptian masses by progressive education appropriate to their customs and occupation so that the people realise their rights and their duties, and that this should

[1] *La Genèse de l'Esprit National Egyptian* by M. Sabry, Paris, 1924, p. 174, n.1 and p. 175.

be done by their own element as far as possible. (This has the true ring of Sheikh Mohammed Abdu's thought.)

The document continues by agreeing that the downfall of Ismail was merited but regretting that it came about by a foreign diplomatic affair. The Egyptian Nationalist Party is outspoken about the situation which followed Ismail's abdication. Thus: "It cannot consider the Government formed by foreign influence, as expressing the wishes and needs of the country. As constituted, this Government has no true Egyptian links and its base is artificial. The Powers alone competed in its formation. The nation counts for nothing. A Khedive reigns in Cairo but the direction of affairs at top level does not emanate from him, nor from his ministry.

"Under such a regime, Egypt, always responsible for the faults of others of which she has had her fill, goes to her downfall. . . . She feels herself to be young enough and strong enough to regenerate her own self. She wishes to. That is why she loudly claims the exercise of her rights, by confiding her interests to the Egyptian National Party composed of capable and proven men. . . .

"Egypt wishes to liberate herself from her debts on condition that the Powers leave her free to apply urgent reforms. The country must be administered by Egyptian personalities of her own choice, without wholly excluding foreign help. She does not always want ministers representing this or the other European influence. . . ."

With a clear statement that Egypt is convinced Europe wishes her well, the National Party continue by making "a solemn appeal to the cabinets of the free and civilised world", which plea, they say, "will certainly be heard because it will be understood by the people". The pith of it is a request for protection against arbitrary attempts on the life and rights of the National Party leaders directed against them by present or future Egyptian Governments, thus allowing them to render service to their country without fear of being molested.

"Under that guarantee," they say, "loyally asked and loyally given, all members of the Nationalist Party will publicly appeal to the nation, accepting responsibility for what they do." A special plea is addressed by the National Party to: "the Prince Chancellor Bismark who recognises the great principle of anatomy of nations, that he might undertake to plead its cause before the tribunals of the nations." The National Party then begged the Powers to take no definite measures contrary to the contents of this manifesto without consulting them.

Among much that is general in this document there is at least one internal demand that is particular. It is the demand that the estates of the Khedival family become the property of the Egyptian state with the exception of what was personally inherited, i.e. that all Ismail's acquired lands should become state-owned. As is well-known, nearly eighty years passed before this demand was fulfilled. In Nasser's revolutions of 1952 no exceptions were made and the ruling family lost all their lands most of which were later distributed to the peasants. Feeling can bank up in three generations.

While Arabi and his colleagues were giving expression to the feelings which stirred within them, the European advisers to the Egyptian government were getting down to some actual reforms. The international commission was formed to grapple with the liquidation of the debt. Nearly 50 per cent of the state revenue was put aside to help pay it off. The interest due to the creditors was reduced from 5 per cent to 4 per cent. Some unfair taxes which had been conjured up during Ismail's reign, were abolished. These were most valuable and needed measures.

There were two points, however, which helped to alienate the nationalist element, perhaps minor points viewed in the general bustle inherent in the putting of a house in order, but to the forces gathering round Ahmed Arabi they were important. Only a small sum was put aside towards repayment of government debts incurred to Egyptian land owners, in comparison to the proportionally larger amounts handed over to European creditors. There may have been some technical reason for this, but whether the technical reason for doing so was more important than the psychological reason for not doing so, is an open question.

The other point which was to lead to difficulties, was the inclusion of Osman Rifki in the Cabinet as Minister of War. He was of Circassian origin and followed the well-known path of promoting officers of his own element rather than Egyptians. He also reduced the years of conscription from five to four, a measure popular enough with many a peasant whose vision was limited to his family and field, but others, who were beginning to think on national lines, felt that this shorter service would mean that the ordinary conscript of Egyptian race would never have time to show his ability and become an officer.

One of Osman Rifki's measures which angered Arabi was an order for soldiers (including those of Arabi's regiment) to leave their military duties for a time, and dredge or dig canals. Arabi refused to send his men to this task.

It is hard to untangle the threads of bravery and fear, of daring and of dread, which co-existed in Arabi's character. Some people writing of those times emphasize one characteristic, some the other, according to the party or personality they chose to back. Several represent him as motivated from now on by a panic for his own safety, aware of little but the personal danger he may have brought upon himself by running contrary to authority. Therefore they view each move which appeared daring, as being an effort to keep final punishment at bay by wild action.

Arabi was at the house of one of his fellow officers one evening when rumour reached him that he and a colleague of his were to be dismissed from the army. While there, a message came from another of his confederate officers asking Arabi to call and see him. When he did so he heard the same news. In view of this they decided to go straight to the Prime Minister with a petition, charging Osman Rifki with unjust behaviour and requesting a full inquiry into the matter of promotion.

On arrival at the Ministry they were shown into an outer room where they waited while the Minister read their petition in an adjacent room. Presently he came out and indicated the gravity of their request by telling them it was a matter which might well involve swinging from a rope. He then asked the Colonels that if their intentions were to change the ministry, with whom could they replace it? "Is Egypt a woman who has borne but eight sons and then become barren?" replied Arabi. That he was alluding to the Prime Minister and the seven members of his cabinet, was evident. The Prime Minister was angry but said that the matter would be looked into. So the Colonels took their departure.[2]

Probably no one this side of the grave will ever know what went on at the discussions or in the minds of the people involved during the following fortnight. The rumours and counter rumours are reflected in the few writers who attempted to record it at the time or within living memory of the events. Some say that the Prime

[2] See *Arabi's Memoirs, Secret History of the English Occupation of Egypt* by W. Scawen Blunt, Fisher Unwin, 1907, p. 136 and *Tarajim mashahir al-sharq.*, by J. Zaidan, 1902, p. 244 (Cairo).

Minister tried unsuccessfully to get the Colonels to withdraw their petition; others, that the Khedive was most displeased with Arabi, and gave his Prime Minister to understand that unless he did something decisive to deal with the matter, his own loyalties would be called in question.

Others again say that the Khedive really wished to get rid of the Prime Minister himself, so tried to ferment an open quarrel between the Colonels and the Ministry. Be that as it may the upshot was that a Council of Ministers was called to discuss the situation. The English and French Controllers were not admitted to this meeting, where it was decided to arrest the Colonels and try them by Court Martial, then investigate their grievances afterwards.

It is reported that Arabi and his friends had an ally in the ministerial circle who had promised to inform them if he ever felt their lives to be in danger. News of the Council's decision certainly reached their ears in no time, and they were able to make a counter plan. If the Colonels were summoned to the Ministry of War and did not emerge safely after two hours, the officers and men of their own regiments were to march on the Ministry and release them by force. Another regiment quartered at Tura also threw in their lot with this scheme.

Sure enough, a summons to the Ministry of War did come to the officers, but the pill they were intended to swallow was so coated in sugar that it could only be called a trap. They were asked to come and plan a military procession which was to be part of the celebrations connected with the forthcoming wedding of the Princess Gamila. The Colonels came and were at once arrested. They and their followers firmly believed that the arrest would have led to the summary disposal of themselves after the manner only too well known in the time of Ismail: a quick struggle and a splash into the Nile, or instant deportation to the White Nile Province, followed by silence for ever.

Present historians can only surmise whether those who arrested them did, or did not, intend to give them a fair trial and look into their grievances. The question must be left at the Judgment Seat, though a human jury might well be swayed by the odd steps taken to ensure the arrest. Anyhow, a trial of some sort did begin. But it did not proceed far. For with great noise and commotion a large number of the Colonels' own men broke into the Ministry and into the Court Room. In those days the Ministry was in the Kasr al Nil

Palace, so well known to generations of British soldiers, as the Kasr al Nil Barracks, where they were quartered throughout the British military occupation of Egypt.

On that day, 1 February 1881, the Egyptian peasant-soldier had the run of the place. In the course of releasing his officers he took the opportunity of knocking about his Minister of War, who had to escape through a window. And then, finally to express his feelings, he kicked the furniture around to his heart's content. No plot could have succeeded better. At the Colonel's command, the regiments turned their back on the disorderly scene, re-formed and marched to their barracks with bands playing, drums beating and their ex-prisoner officers at their head.

The great question of what to do next was a hard one for the authorities to answer. A policy of force against Arabi and his men was difficult to carry out, for all regiments stationed near Cairo were in sympathy with the Nationalists. Therefore, after much cogitation, the Khedive Tewfik sent for the Colonels and told them that Osman Rifki was dismissed and that they were allowed to keep the command of their regiments. On hearing this the Colonels apologised to the Khedive for the manner in which they had conducted the affair, and swore allegiance to him.

Arabi's popularity was now out in the open. Many a country farmer, village headman and local notable was in touch with him to tell him of the support he had in the provinces. They looked on him as one of themselves, as indeed he was. "Al Wahid" he was called—"the unique", or "al Basha batahna"—"our own Pasha". Much of this enthusiasm was straightforward enough. But there were factions which made up to Arabi, now that he was gaining power, so as to further their own schemes of intrigue or to implant their own will on any plans of reform which might be in the offing. It is said that the Khedive encouraged Arabi, in confidence, to consider himself somewhat of a personage, so that he (the Khedive) could use him to oust the Prime Minister whom he was said to dislike. Some of the party pressing for a Constitution thought Arabi would be just the man to help bring it about in such a way as to ensure that their own personal power remained paramount.

At the same time Arabi and his fellow officers felt fundamentally ill at ease. They were beset with spies and, rightly or wrongly, they felt that their lives were in danger. Every incident or turn of events was thought to signify more than met the eye, by the Khedive, the Prime Minister, Arabi and the army and the European Consuls.

Arabi said in later years that he knew none of the Consuls at this time but he had heard that the French was the most influential, so before he had gone with his petition to the Prime Minister, he had written to the French Consul, Baron de Ring, explaining the position of the nationalists and asking him to let the other Consuls know that no danger would ensue for the foreign communities. It so happened that Baron de Ring espoused Arabi's cause with warmth and had frequent consultations with him. Writers who viewed Arabi's aspirations with sympathy throughout, felt that Baron de Ring was an understanding and disinterested man, but writers with other views said that he had a quarrel with the Prime Minister and that his aim in advancing Arabi was to overthrow the former through working on Arabi's distrust.

Eventually de Ring's influence with Arabi was looked on as an unwarranted complication and the Khedive, backed by the English, asked France to remove him. But many Frenchmen were concerned about the nature of French influence in Egypt. Monsieur de Fréycinet, who became French Prime Minister in 1882, wrote thus of Arabi and the army: "The appointment of Osman Rifki was a bungle: it would have been better, in view of the state of feeling at the time, to have given the portfolio of war to an officer of Egyptian nationality."[3] And again: "The year 1882 found us in the position of creditors, nervous for the future of our rights. This question of money, today we can admit it, unduly inspired the action of our diplomacy. The praiseworthy anxiety to protect our own interests, had at times encroached upon the general and permanent interests of France. . . ."[4]

The Army's taste for successful defiance, coupled with incidents over which the authorities showed the reverse of tact, created a volcanic atmosphere during this summer of 1881.

A soldier was killed in a street accident in July. His fellow soldiers got it into their heads that his death had not been wholly accidental. They carried his body to the palace, defied the guards and went in with it. The leading spirits stood a trial and were punished. Intrigue was everywhere. A group of nineteen officers accused one of the Colonels associated with Arabi of various charges. When these charges were investigated they could not be proven, so the

[3] *Le Question d'Egypte* by de Fréycinet, Paris, 1905, p. 193.
[4] *Souvenirs* 1878-1893 by de Fréycinet, Paris 1914, 9th edition, p. 216.

officers who raised them were dismissed. Not long afterwards, however, there were the same men, back in their old positions. Such affairs pacified none of the factions.

A Commission was set up to investigate the original grievances of the army and Arabi served on it, but in the course of this, "his language to the Minister of War was very disrespectful", records Lord Cromer.[5]

What finally convinced Arabi that action was again imperative was the appointment of one, Daoud Pasha Yeghan, a brother-in-law of the Khedive, as Minister of War, who was well known to view their persons and their cause with distaste. One of the first things this new Minister did, was to order Arabi and the Colonel closest to him, away from Cairo to Alexandria and Damietta respectively. Arabi and his friend felt that this would be a strategic blow to their unity of purpose—as indeed we may guess it was meant to be. They held a hurried consultation with their leading civilian allies, and decided that a full-scale demonstration should take place immediately. According to Arabi, the next morning he wrote a letter stating his demands and saying that he and his followers would march to Abdin Palace there to receive the Khedive's answer. The reason given for going to Abdin rather than to the Ismailia Palace, where Tewfik lived, was that Abdin was his public residence and Arabi did not wish to alarm the ladies of the household.

When the Khedive arrived at Abdin on September 9th he found the Army occupying the square. He called on Arabi to dismount and to put up his sword, which he did. Then Arabi made his three demands to the Khedive, that the Ministry should be dismissed; that a representative chamber should be formed; and that the army strength should be raised to 18,000 men. "I am Khedive of the country and shall do as I please," said Tewfik, and Arabi replied, "We are not slaves and shall never from this day forth be inherited."

The Khedive turned and went back into the palace. Presently the British Consul-General at Alexandria came out with an interpreter. (He was in charge as Sir Edward Malet, Consul-General in Egypt, was absent on leave.) He asked why, being a soldier, Arabi demanded a Parliament. "To put an end to arbitrary rule," answered Arabi, pointing to the crowd of citizens supporting him behind the soldiers. "But we will bring a British army," said the Consul-General. Much discussion took place between them,

[5] *Modern Egypt*, op. cit., p. 142.

punctuated with six or seven visits to the palace, until finally Arabi was informed that the Khedive had agreed to all.[6]

The various eye witness reports of what took place at Abdin Palace that day vary considerably. The above account is taken from Arabi's own words. *The Times* correspondent had the impression that the Cairo crowds, which Arabi saw as earnest supporters, were just riff-raff lolling around eating monkey nuts and out to see the fun. Mr. Auckland Colvin writes that he urged Tewfik to arrest Arabi, there and then, but that the Khedive hesitated and missed the psychological moment.

Monsieur Charmes, a French journalist, certainly drew on his imagination when describing the visit of Arabi and his companions to the palace that evening to thank the Khedive. According to him they kissed Tewfik's feet, made him the most sacred oaths of loyalty, knelt before him, their heads upon the ground ("trainèrent leurs fronts sur le parquet") then went out to prepare fresh revolutionary schemes. This seemingly eyewitness account would be more convincing had the author not gone on to say that these events had taken place so rapidly and with such profound secrecy that no one in Cairo knew of them save those who found themselves by chance in Abdin Square. "No witness assisted at these strange scenes,"[7] he adds. But this had not deterred him from a detailed description of what took place inside the palace.

Mr. Auckland Colvin's[8] memorandum to Lord Granville at the Foreign Office is of interest on account of his deductions on the nature of Egyptian nationalism. He was then the British Controller in Egypt. "There seems to me no reason to believe that anyone but the officers themselves are concerned in the movement. . . . It was a purely military demonstration, the work of men who think they hold the country in their own hands. . . .

"It is hopeless to appeal to their self-interest. Nothing so much impressed me yesterday as the profound unconsciousness on the part of all the officers of the immense danger to themselves which they are incurring. They spoke like men convinced that they would be allowed to settle their own disputes with the Government, that Europe had neither the right nor the wish to interfere. This makes it impossible to work on the instinct of self-preservation. They are

[6] *Secret History*, op. cit., p. 149.
[7] *Revue des Deux Mondes*, 15 August 1883, p. 764.
[8] He was knighted in 1882.

blinded to the consequences of their acts. They believe they are
engaged in working out the liberties of their country; and that
the method they have adopted is justified by the circumstances in
which the country is placed.''

During the months which led up to the acquiring of power by
Ahmed Arabi, Mohammed Abdu was in touch with the Nationalists,
though he by no means approved of their plans. So at first it was
not a matter of close consultation, but of outspoken words on both
sides. Arabi genuinely thought the time was ripe for shaking off
the shackles of despotic rule and starting some form of parliamentary
government representing the people. Mohammed Abdu clung to
his conviction that the next years should be devoted to the education
of the people preparatory to national development in due course.

He strongly counselled Arabi to be moderate in his demands
and patient about results, saying that by so doing he would gain
more in the end. He feared violence might shipwreck his cherished
plans for gradual reform from within, and he must have guessed,
with far greater clarity than Arabi could command, that a military
uprising would not be allowed to succeed.

Yet, as time spun out, showing daily that the Khedive was more
and more influenced by England and France and that all three
were closing in on Arabi, Mohammed Abdu made the decision
to throw in his lot with the Nationalists. It must have been a counsel
of despair which he administered to himself, for he still felt in his
heart that somehow they were wrong. But as the situation was clearly
becoming a two-sided contest—England, France and the Khedive
on one side, with Arabi and his following on the other side—
Mohammed Abdu felt that he now had no choice. Notwithstanding
that he saw all their failings, and felt the uneasiness still rife within
him, one course alone was clear to Mohammed Abdu. Arabi represented something which could be called Egypt, and the others
did not. If they were going to oppose Arabi, then he, Mohammed
Abdu, should be beside Arabi. But it must have cost him dear to
do so, for he could see into the future more clearly than most.

The officers gathered secretly in Abdin barracks one day to
take an oath of loyalty to Egypt and it was Mohammed Abdu
who administered the oath. The soldiers now ceased arguing with
him, instead they often turned to him for advice. In his capacity

of editor of *Egyptian Events* he was able to focus what he thought were the sound points of the military party, through the columns of his paper.

It certainly looked as if the military demonstration outside Abdin Palace on 9 September had been a great step forward in Egypt's effort to realise her national personality. The incident had caught the imagination of thousands of Egyptians and was sympathetically regarded by not a few Europeans living in the land. People of the three main faiths—Moslems, Jews and Christians—whose home was Egypt, were also united by what seemed the dawn of a new liberation for the Egyptian spirit. It was "literally true that in the streets of Cairo, men stopped each other, though strangers, to embrace and rejoice together," as said an eye witness.[9]

These propitious sights, however, but reflected the sunny seas in which the ship of state found herself sailing, with a blue sky above. Beneath her were many rocks and her keel was, even then, bumping against them continually. Arabi and the Prime Minister differed on several points. The Minister felt that a soldier should interfere less in political affairs. So Arabi was ordered with his regiment, to be transferred to Ras al Wadi, near Zagazig. He obeyed, as any Colonel in normal circumstances would do. It is likely that he really wished to show a spirit of co-operation though the move was to his disadvantage. But the send-off he had at Cairo railway station was hardly the type usually accorded to those on a normal regimental transfer.

Crowds gathered on the platform, speeches and poems were delivered, flowers and sweetmeats were circulated for the benefit of all and the ubiquitous water-carrier was there to quench the thirst of the multitudes. Arabi leant from the window of the train and replied with a speech in which he said how European revolutions to win liberty had been gained through blood-shed and civil strife, yet thanks to the Khedive Tewfik, present day Egypt had been able to take a big step towards her liberty, with no violence. "We have won because we are united," he said. "My advice to you is to keep that unity till the end. Long live the Khedive, the giver of liberty! Long live the army, the seeker of liberty!"[10]

The populace must have enjoyed the scene to capacity. It was early October, hot enough still for them to relish the drinks of cool

[9] *Secret History*, op. cit., p. 153.
[10] *The Awakening of Modern Egypt*, by M. Rifaat, Longmans, 1947, p. 186.

water. The clink of the brass saucers, which the dispenser of such drinks manipulates as he threads his way through the crowd, would have made a pleasant incidental noise to the rolling Arabic phrases of the poems, which can so move even an unlettered Egyptian peasant.

An Egyptian crowd of this sort carries with it an extenuated family atmosphere unparalleled by most other crowds. It is composed of greybeards, grandmothers lacking front teeth, babies who can just walk, babies who cannot walk, eager young men and shrill-voiced girls—all outgoing and cheerful. Arabi must have pulled out of Cairo station with this scene ringing in his head and heart. The populace had an intimate touch with him at this time. Visitors to his house had to find their way through a throng of people both in the street outside the door and in the outer hall. All were there with pleas of some sort to be brought personally to Arabi for redress. One can well imagine that some of the tales told were false and some were real, some were tales concocted round incidents of pique and others were of true and grievous wounds. But all suppliants alike must have felt that Arabi could help them.

In the meantime, the news of events in Egypt had caused some puzzlement in Constantinople. The Sultan Abdel Hamid had reason to wonder what was afoot. Was it a good thing as far as he was concerned or was it a bad thing? Should he investigate? If so, should the mission be military or civil? This in its turn produced a buzz of diplomatic activity in Europe. Both French and English Governments thought it would be most unwise of the Sultan to send troops to Egypt. If even a single Turkish General went, France thought, it might lead to a Turkish interference embarrassing for Europe, though England considered that, with French and English consent, a single Turkish General might well be dispatched. For the sake of a united front, however, both Ambassadors to the Porte were instructed to stop the Sultan from sending a Turkish General if he showed signs of wishing to do so.

The Sultan did send a mission, however, consisting of two civilian envoys who arrived on the Egyptian scene in early October to the pained surprise of England and France who capped the move by sending a gunboat each to patrol the waters off Alexandria.

It so happened that Arabi was travelling by train from Zagazig to Tel al Kebir when he found himself in a carriage with a stranger.

They exchanged compliments and names, as is the custom in Egypt, and the stranger added that he was on his way to Suez to embark on pilgrimage to Mecca. He did not mention any other reason for being in the country, but his name told Arabi that this stranger was indeed one of the Sultan's special envoys to Egypt. Arabi took the opportunity of mentioning the fact that he was loyal to the Sultan as head of their religion.

Shortly afterwards the envoys left and the gunboats left, but not without much manoeuvring between England and France and Turkey as to which should leave first. Later on, the envoy who had met Arabi in the train sent him a Koran from Jeddah, and on his return to Constantinople wrote to say he had put in a good word for him with the Sultan.

While at Zagazig, Arabi continued to make speeches which excited the populace. He did not express enmity towards Europeans as such, but he was reported as being outspoken against the employment of Europeans in Egypt. These were clearly different points to him personally, but there must have been many in his enthusiastic audiences to whom the difference was less clear.

His speeches appeared in the Arabic press and were avidly read. So the European press of Egypt responded in kind, with language calculated to insult. It is interesting to ponder these facts in the light of an account written by Mr. Auckland Colvin of an interview he had with Arabi and two of his fellow officers on 1 November 1881. Arabi started with an historical introduction on how Egypt had been physically oppressed by the rule of the Mamelukes and the house of Mohammed Ali, under which rulers, he said, "a liberated slave was a freer man than a freeborn Arab."

"He then went on at great length," wrote Mr. Colvin, "to explain that men come of one common stock and had equal rights of personal liberty and security. The development of this theme took some considerable time, and was curious in its naive treatment, but it evidently was the general outcome of the speaker's laboured thoughts, and was the expression not of rhetorical periods, but of conviction.

"Passing on to the bearing of his reasoning on facts, he said that on the 1st February the Circassian rule (by which he meant the arbitrary Turkish regime) had fallen in Egypt, on the 9th September the necessity of substituting for it the era of law and justice had been recognised and established. It was for law and justice that he and the army contended. He disclaimed in the plainest words the desire to get rid of Europeans, whether as employees or residents; he spoke of them as the necessary instructors of the people. . . . They had no wish to question the need of Europeans in the administration; on the contrary, if more were required let them come. . . . The impression left on my mind was that Arabi, who spoke with great moderation, calmness and conciliation, is sincere and resolute, but is not a practical man. The exposition, not the execution, of ideas is his strength."[11]

During 1881 Arabi had made friends with that remarkable Englishman, Wilfrid Scawen Blunt. He was grandfather of the present Lord Lytton and was a poet, traveller, orientalist and breeder of Arab horses. When not in England, seeing to his extensive Sussex estates, he was usually living in a small house some eight miles out of Cairo on the edge of the desert, with his wife, Lady Anne Blunt. Mohammed Abdu was among their Egyptian friends who often visited them in their home, surrounded by orange trees and the stables of the Arab blood stock. Blunt espoused the cause of Arabi with the full impact of his warm-hearted if hot-headed enthusiasm. His views were often a source of embarrassment to the British government, and opinions differ as to whether, in the long run, they were a source of embarrassment to Arabi. But if this was so, if Arabi was at a later date politically misled by Blunt, he, Arabi, was only conscious of the sincerity and disinterestedness of Blunt's friendship.

In December 1881, Mohammed Abdu, Arabi and Wilfrid Blunt co-operated in drawing up a document entitled the Programme of the National Party of Egypt. It was reasonable and conciliatory in tone. They stated that the National Party fully recognised the services rendered to Egypt by the Governments of England and France, and they were aware that all freedom and justice they had obtained in the past had been due to them. "For this they tender them their thanks," the document reads. "They recognise the European Control as a necessity of their financial position, and the continuance of it as the best guarantee of their prosperity. . . . They look, nevertheless, upon the existing order of things as in its nature temporary, and avow it as their hope gradually to redeem the country out of the hands of its creditors. Their object is, some day to see Egypt entirely in Egyptian hands. . . .

[11] Quoted by Lord Cromer in *Modern Egypt*, op. cit., p. 163.

"They trust in the sympathy of those of the nations of Europe which enjoy the blessing of self-government to aid Egypt in gaining for itself that blessing; but they are aware that no nation ever yet achieved liberty except by its own endeavours; and they are resolved to stand firm in the position they have won, trusting to God's help if all other be denied them."

On 20 December Mr. Blunt forwarded this document to Mr. Gladstone with a covering letter in which he said that he could not understand that these were sentiments to be deplored or actions to be crushed by an English Liberal Government, but that the lovers of Western progress should rather congratulate themselves on this strange and unlooked-for sign of political life in a land which had hitherto been reproached by them as the least thinking portion of the stagnant East. "You Sir, I think," wrote Mr. Blunt, "once expressed to me your belief that the nations of the East could only regenerate themselves by a spontaneous resumption of their lost national *Will* and behold in Egypt that *Will* has arisen and is now struggling to find words which may persuade Europe of its existence."

Mr. Gladstone's reply was in general terms, but he permitted himself to say that unless there were to be a sad failure of good sense on one, or both, or all sides, they would be enabled to bring the question to a favourable issue. The Prime Minister's private secretary, a personal friend of Wilfrid Blunt, also wrote:

"You may imagine that the alleged national character of the movement necessarily commends itself to Mr. Gladstone with his well-known sympathy with young nationalists struggling for independence. The great crux (I am of course only speaking of myself, and with a strong consciousness of ignorance) seems to be, how to favour such a movement with due regard to the responsibilities in which we have been involved, and the vested interests which are at stake. Every alternative seems to be beset with insuperable objections and insurmountable difficulties. I can only say that if you can do anything towards finding a solution for these difficulties you will be doing a great work for Egypt, for the country, and for the present Government. . . ."[12]

This letter hardly needs the alteration of more than six words to be apposite to a dozen situations in Asia and Africa from the day it was written till now.

[12] For the above information see *Secret History*, op. cit., pp. 173 and 556.

Between Mr. Blunt's letter to Mr. Gladstone and its reply, the year 1881 drew to a close—a year of much mistrust. As a postscript to it the Egyptian trade report of 1881, compiled by the British Consulate, contained a short statement that trade between Great Britain and Egypt had lessened that year and trade between Egypt and Russia had increased.[13]

[13] See *The Times*, 2 September 1882.

CHAPTER VI

A NOTE, A HOME AND A PLOT

EARLY in January 1882 Arabi was nominated Under-Secretary of State for War. There seem to have been several reasons behind this move, emanating from various sources and most of them at variance with one another. To give him enough rope to hang himself was one reason; to train him in the responsibilities of office was another; to separate him from his soldiers was a third; and a fourth reasoning was that as he seemed to have the power anyway, why not legitimise it?

In the meantime the Governments of France and England were in close collaboration about their agreed necessity of doing something. Lord Granville and Monsieur Gambetta, from their respective Foreign Offices, were sending communications across the Channel to each other, across the road to each other's Ambassadors, and across the Mediterranean to their representatives in Egypt. Monsieur Gambetta was the leading spirit and Lord Granville tagged along manfully in spite of the fact that one despatch from France arrived on December 24th and Sir Edward Malet's advice had to be asked for from Cairo on December 26th, making a very short Christmas holiday. But to do Monsieur Gambetta justice, his New Year's Day must have been a busy one, for his draft of what the two Governments might together say to Egypt was delivered in London on 2 January 1882.

Gambetta is reported to have said: "I am in agreement with England. Europe is indifferent and will let us act. I have prepared, on the coast of Provence, an invasion force [un corps de débarquement] of six thousand marines, which can be thrown into Egypt in a few days."[1]

On January 8th the English and French Consuls-General in Egypt delivered to the Khedive the Joint Note from their respective governments.

"The English and French Governments," it stated, "consider the maintenance of His Highness on the throne, as alone able to guarantee, for the present and future, the good order and development of general prosperity in Egypt, in which France and Great Britain

[1] *Souvenirs* 1878-1893, C. de Friycinet, Paris, 9th edition, 1914, p. 212.

are equally interested. The two Governments being closely associated in the resolve to guard by their united efforts against all cause of complication, internal or external, which might menace the order of things established in Egypt, do not doubt that the assurance publicly given of their formal intentions in this respect will tend to avert the dangers to which the Government of the Khedive might be exposed, and which would certainly find England and France united to oppose them.

"They are convinced that His Highness will draw from this assurance the confidence and strength which he requires to direct the destinies of Egypt and his people."

The effect of this Joint Note was expressed by contemporary observers in a variety of ways but with one meaning. Sir Edward Malet himself said that it had, at least temporarily, alienated England from all Egyptian confidence, as it was considered that England had definitely thrown in her lot with France, and that France was determined ultimately to intervene from motives in connection with her Tunisian campaign.[2]

The Fortnightly Review (July 1882), published an article by Mr. John Morley in which he said: "At Cairo, the Note fell like a bombshell. Nobody had expected such a declaration and nobody there was aware of any reason why it should have been launched. What was felt, was that so serious a step on such delicate ground, could not have been taken without deliberate calculation nor without some grave intention.

"The Note was therefore taken to mean that the Sultan was to be thrust still farther in the background; that the Khedive was to become more plainly the puppet of England and France; and that Egypt would, sooner or later, in some shape or other, be made to share the disastrous fate of Tunis."

As for the Egyptian Prime Minister—"Quelle boulette!" he exclaimed. "Ils n'auraient pu trouver mieux pour nous perdre."[3] He at least was lost, for the Chamber of Notables requested the Khedive to change the Ministry, and the Prime Minister was dismissed.

On 31 January Monsieur Gambetta resigned, and Monsieur de Fréycinet took his place at the Quai d'Orsay.

In the new Egyptian Ministry Arabi found himself Minister

[2] Parliamentary Papers, Affairs of Egypt, Malet to Granville, 6 February 1882.
[3] See *La Genèse de l'Esprit National Egyptian* by M. Sabry, p. 203.

of War and a Pasha. It was in this month, February 1882, that
Lady Gregory (the second wife of Sir William Gregory, once
Governor of Ceylon and a staunch Liberal Irishman) paid a visit
to Arabi's wife and mother, in his home in Cairo. What Lady
Gregory had to say was published by Kegan Paul that same year
in a twelve-page pamphlet called "Arabi and his Household"
(price 2d).

She gives her impression of Arabi's looks. "In appearance Arabi
is a tall, strongly built man, his face is grave, almost stern, but his
smile is very pleasant. His photographs reproduce the sternness
but not the smile, and are, I believe, partly responsible for the
ready belief which the absurd tales of his ferocity and bloodthirsti-
ness have gained."

Arabi had married the daughter of a nurse of Al Hami Pasha,
a great-grandson of Mohammed Ali the Great. They had moved
some little time before to a new house, large and dilapidated looking.
Lady Gregory describes the simplicity of this establishment, so
as to counteract the rumours then current in England, of the luxu-
rious style of living indulged in by Arabi. It was being said (with
the exact detail so often met in rumour) that he had lately spent
£120 on new carpets. Lady Gregory eyed the carpets carefully during
her visit and recorded that, if they had cost £120 all she could say
was that Arabi had struck a very bad bargain.

Lady Gregory made this call in the company of Wilfrid Blunt's
wife, Lady Anne, who spoke fluent Arabic. The ladies were received
by Arabi's wife who had a pleasant, intelligent expression but
was worn and worried. Only five children had survived of the
fourteen born to her and Arabi.

Her long dress of green silk had a train. Her husband hated it,
she explained, but she felt she should have something smart to
wear when visiting the Khedive's wife and other ladies.

Some time before, Lady Gregory had visited the then Prime
Minister's wife, Madame Sherif, who had told her that when Madame Arabi had called on her she had taken the opportunity, as
Prime Minister's wife, to speak severely to Madame Arabi telling
her to go home and make her husband behave better and stop his
stupidities. Madame Arabi had cried and promised to do her best.
So, in spite of the green silk dress, her visits to great ladies had
not been all happy ones.

An old woman with white hair dressed in country clothes was

introduced to the English ladies. Unlike Arabi's puzzled wife, this old lady was full of energy and vivacity. "I am only a fellaha, but I am the Mother of Ahmed Arabi," she said as she showed off an oleograph of her son, in startling colours.

Arabi's wife spoke to the English ladies of the time when he and the two other Colonels were rescued from their court-martial in Kasr al Nil barracks. She had hired a carriage and driven to the palace to try and get news of them but could gather nothing and returned home. That evening her baby girl was born. At the moment of her birth came the news of Arabi's release by the soldiers. So the baby was called Bushra, meaning Good Tidings, and was said to be her father's favourite. She was now brought in for the visitors to view—tiny, thin, with huge black eyes.

The English ladies left with expressions of hope that they might meet the Arabi household again. "If God wills," replied his wife. "They say the Christian powers want to do something to my husband. I don't understand it at all. We can't get on without the Christians or they without us. Why can't we all live in peace together?"

A few weeks later, before the Gregorys left Cairo, another visit was paid to the Arabi family. This time Lady Gregory found them all sadder and more anxious. Even the old mother, so confident earlier in the pride of her son, could now only speak of her fear for him. "I can do nothing but pray for him all the time. There are many who wish him evil. . . . I keep even the water that he drinks locked up. But, say all I can, I cannot frighten him or make him take care of himself—he always says, 'God will preserve me.'"

Arabi's wife said she would have liked to send their little boy, Hassan, to one of the Christian schools in Cairo to learn English. "But how can I send him where he would hear his father spoken ill of?" was her comment.

During these early months of 1882 Arabi was in contact with Ferdinand de Lesseps, President of the "Compagnie Universelle de Canal Maritime de Suez", to whom Arabi had promised the concession of a sweet water canal to run parallel to the big canal and be connected with the Nile. This became the sweet water canal, as it exists today. De Lesseps and Arabi always counted on each other as friends. There were Americans then in Egypt who also viewed his cause with favour.

One such was Mr. Wolf, United States Consul-General, who gave a banquet on 22 February 1882, to celebrate the anniversary of Washington's birthday. Arabi and Ferdinand de Lesseps were both invited to attend, together with other members of the Egyptian cabinet. This particular occasion was described in an obscure little book published in America (Appleton & Co.) in 1884, and sold for 20 cents. It is called *The Three Prophets*, by Colonel C. Chaillé Long, who describes himself as "ex-chief of staff to Gordon in Africa, ex-United States Consular Agent in Alexandria etc. etc." American contemporary opinions on Egyptian affairs in general, and on Arabi in particular, were as strongly divided as they were in England. Colonel Chaillé Long's point of view is clearly seen by his personal description of Arabi.

He is "a tall, big, strong, heavy-looking fellah, wears his fez thrown back upon his head, and when not conversing keeps his eyes closed, opening them at intervals with whites upturned, producing a very ugly and disagreeable impression of hypocrisy and fanaticism. His colour is the dirty yellow common to the fellah of Lower Egypt. His head is rather pointed, with large mouth and thick lips, which move incessantly in mumbling the verses of the Koran, while his fingers are running over in ceaseless count the chaplet which he holds in the right hand."

The Consuls-General of England and France both refused their invitations to this banquet in honour of George Washington's memory because of the proposed presence of Arabi. They had asked the advice of Colonel Chaillé Long in this delicate matter and he had emphatically said that they should absent themselves. A graphic account of the dinner and speeches, from the pen of Colonel Chaillé Long, leads one to suppose that he himself accepted an invitation to the dinner in spite of advising others to keep away. Monsieur de Lesseps gave a speech in which he drew a parallel between the young American Union and the old land of Egypt, who he said, were both holding high the standard of liberty for their peoples.

The Times of 14 February 1882, carried a long comment on the current Egyptian situation.

"The Egyptians. . . may prefer to govern themselves, even if they do not govern well. Little can be said of such a desire as long as it does not lead to any breach of international faith. Present things, no doubt, are galling. A friend drew a lively picture of them to me this morning," writes the author of the article. "Imagine yourself," he said, "an Egyptian coming back to this country after seven years' absence. You arrive at Alexandria and find the great port managed by a harbourmaster who is an English sailor. You land your boxes and you find yourself in a custom-house con- trolled by an English post-office official. You go to Cairo by the main railway, which you find administered by an Anglo-Indian and a French railway *employé*. You send a telegram to your friends by lines superintended by an English telegraphist, or you write by a postal service managed by another ex-official of the English Post Office. You want to go to the Upper Nile and you are forced to use a steamboat monopoly established by Thomas Cook & Co. You go into the country and you find old friends lost in the toils of a big money-lending English company. You ask why your fellow-countrymen are not better taught; you find the Public Debt absorbs all the money which might go for schools and canals. I could go on with my instances, but I have given you reason enough were you an Egyptian who loves his country to throw in his lot with the National Party."

It could be said of England abroad, that in conscientious anxiety to push through good schemes, she has sometimes pushed aside the very people whom the schemes were meant to benefit. She has then been grieved by the results. The fault lies, not in the material good achieved but in the human cost by which it was achieved. England has so often played a double role. She has been the judge who proclaims the sentence but the provocative agent also, the welfare worker but the tempter as well, the surgeon and the germ-carrier too.

The surgical operation may seem successful, the reforming advice sound and the sentence may be just but this double role does not produce the new greatness in ourselves nor in others so needed by the world today. The outcome is division, not unity.

Feeling in England for and against Arabi was running as high as it was in Egypt. The country was deeply divided. On 6 March, Sir William Gregory took up his pen and addressed a very lengthy letter to the editor of *The Times*.

Gregory was then a man of sixty-five. He had been an active politician of many interests who had often turned those interests with enthusiasm to the public good. The best of his art collection is in the National Gallery. As well as taking a lead in questions of the state's responsibility to art, he was an acknowledged expert on the turf. He had been a well-loved Governor of Ceylon where he had given thought to many sides of the island's life, from the cultivation of tea and coffee to the preservation of antiquities. But above all, he was a man imbued with a love of the human race.

Sir William knew Egypt well and it was from there that he wrote this letter of which the following are extracts: "I can take it upon myself to say, after making the most searching and impartial enquiries, that no threats have been made by Arabi to anyone upon any subject whatever, and that the army—that is, the soldiers themselves—are under as good and as strict discipline as they have ever been, very different, indeed, from what I can remember them. I will moreover venture to say that more military outrages have been committed in London alone in one month than have been committed in all Egypt since the famous 9th of September—the day of the supremacy of the colonels—and yet the English Army is not represented as being in a state of insubordination. . . . I do not at all desire to write up the present Egyptian Government as perfect, or to express any strong feeling of security as regards the future march of events. I guard myself especially against doing so. History tells us that revolutions are not prone to halt, but I contend that we are in a most difficult position, and that we must make the best of it. . . .

"Under the former *régime* France was everything in Egypt, the word of Napoleon III was law, the Khedive was thoroughly French in his instincts and ideas. French was the predominant language of the Court and Ministers. French operas, French furniture, French novels, French functionaries and French ballet girls reigned supreme, for the favour of Ismail was the favour of the land. All this is over now. The present party is profoundly hostile to Ismail, and what he favoured is their antipathy. Arabic and not French is their language. They have no weakness for Offenbach's music or for the ballet. . . .

"It is well that those who incessantly attack the present men should have in mind that their writings are carefully reproduced in that portion of the Egyptian Press which is unfavourable to England; indeed, I may say, throughout it. Is it likely that Arabi should feel well-disposed to England and Englishmen when he reads that a person in Sir Samuel Baker's high position proposes to send him to Constantinople, which means a good deal more than a mere trip to the Golden Horn, though how Sir Samuel is to carry out his proposal is more than I can understand?

"Is it likely that any feeling, save one of amazement and horror, should pervade Egyptians when they are informed by their news-papers, that the one man essentially venerated through their country should, according to the recommendations of a Christian clergyman, the minister of 'God, the compassionate and merciful', be 'blown from a gun'? It is a pity not to record his name, the Rev. Dr. Badger. But these are individual opinions, it will be said. No doubt to us that is a sufficient answer; but to Egyptians, who erroneously suppose that such opinions would not, unless approved, be admitted into the most influential journals, the answer is unintelligible. . . .

"We may still do much to regain their confidence and goodwill. I will venture to say that 90 out of every 100 of my countrymen are not aware of the injustice under which the Egyptians are labour-ing. The stately palaces built by Europeans and by those who have obtained European nationality, in many instances by very question-able means, are untaxed. The humble dwelling of the Egyptian is taxed at the rate of 12 per cent on the valuation. But this is done through the capitulations with Turkey, it will be said. That is true enough, but it is perfectly easy for England to take the lead and to let the Egyptians know we are taking the lead in endeavouring to relax under proper safeguards this portion of the capitulations.

"Again, let a Maltese, or a Greek, or an Italian practise a trade or mount the box of a hackney coach as a driver, he is exempt from the tax on professions as being under European protection; but an Egyptian striving to earn his bread in a similar manner is taxed in doing so. . . . But it is said that Egyptians are used to this, they do not mind it, they ought to suffer distinctions in order to be humble before their betters. I have actually heard these very reasons given for the maintenance of these discreditable distinctions. Of course, the new Egyptian Government aims at their abolition, and, I should say, of course we should give them our cordial, unfaltering aid in doing so. Let us not, therefore, be too hard on the Egyptians if they show a desire to emancipate themselves from foreign thral-dom. . . .

"I owe many apologies for the length of this and other letters, but it must be borne in mind that the Egyptians have had hardly anyone to place their case before the judgment of the people of England. Had they friends to plead their cause I should have left them in other and abler hands. The births of new Governments are proclaimed with shawms and trumpets, but this national Gov-ernment has hardly a single 'God bless it' from the free countries of Europe, though the whole population of Egypt have raised their hands to Allah in prayer for its duration and success. It has been ushered into the world with averted looks from diplomacy, with tumultuous abuse from officialdom, and with the curses of stock-exchanges. It is no wonder, with such a chorus and with tales of its imaginary misdoings as thick as motes in the sunbeam, that a general impression most averse to it should prevail. I do not attempt to prophesy that it will succeed. The probabilities are adverse. The stars in their courses fight against it. But I believe the leader, Arabi, to be honest and patriotic; I believe the object of the party at present to be honest and patriotic; also, I believe that no policy can be more clear than for England to support the present Egyptian Government, and to be sorry for our own sakes if it fails."

In the meantime, the reports coming in from English official sources in Egypt were dismal in the extreme. Vice-Consuls in the provinces spoke of bands of ruffians who thought the times propitious for the exercise of their trade; banking establishments were loath to lend money, thus playing into the hands of the Jewish and Greek money lenders who charged exorbitant interest; the price of land fell, the price of food rose. Mr. Cookson,[4] the British Consul-General in Alexandria, reported that many men of substance, scenting danger ahead, were thinking better of their alliance with Arabi.

The motif for the month of April was the revealing of a plot. "True in every detail," said some; "Wholly fabricated," thought others. Some time previously Arabi had promoted a number of Egyptian officers over the heads (it is said) of some Turkish and Circassian men. He was now convinced that a party of Circassians had a well-authenticated plot to murder him and other prominent Egyptians.[5]

Lord Cromer, when writing his book, *Modern Egypt*, in 1907, was equally convinced that this plot had been thought up by the Egyptian Nationalists to forestall the wrath of the injured Circassians. He must have come to this conclusion from information passed to him by men on the spot, for Lord Cromer himself was out of Egypt from June 1880 to September 1883.

By the end of April some forty-eight people had been arrested

[4] He was knighted in 1888.

[5] His case was published in *The Nineteenth Century*, 1882, Vol. 12, pp. 969-996, entitled "Instructions to My Counsel".

and tried by Court-Martial in secret. Forty of them, including Osman Rifki, were sentenced to exile for life in the southern Sudan. (Osman Rifki had been Minister of War when Arabi was court-martialled at Kasr al Nil and rescued by his regiment.) This sentence was brought to the Khedive to confirm. He wished to cancel it; the Ministers wished it confirmed; European Consuls and communities in Egypt held many and opposing views. When the controversy reached the ears of the Sultan in Constantinople he thought that he himself should decide on the matter because Osman Rifki was a military General, which rank he had been granted by the hand of the Sultan. The Khedive felt this might be a good way out of the difficulty. But, that the Sultan should thus interfere, caused consternation in the Governments of France and England. Their Consuls in Cairo were told to advise the Khedive to grant the pardon himself, and the quicker the better. He commuted the sentence to exile outside Egypt, but not to the Sudan. This affair drove a deep wedge between Arabi's government and the Khedive, not so much because the Khedive had altered the sentence, as that he had listened to the dictation of the Consuls.

In addition to all this, other plots, rumours and incidents crowded in on Arabi and gave much subject for talk among the European communities of Egypt. My Rowlatt grandparents were now living in England for the sake of their sons' education, so, apart from the papers, they relied on letters from friends in Egypt to keep them abreast of news. Mr. Henry H. Calvert, the British Vice-Consul in Alexandria, was a good correspondent. In a letter dated 8 April 1882 he alluded to another "plot" which caused a great sensation. It appeared that one of Ismail's wives arrived in Alexandria, from sharing her husband's exile. She pleaded ill-health as the reason for her wish to return to Egypt. The Khedive Tewfik sent a medical commission on board to examine into the truth of this statement, but Her Highness would receive none of the medical men. Egyptian Government boats were placed all around the vessel to prevent any of the harem landing. An English lady, resident in Alexandria, went on board to see the Princess, whom she knew, but was not allowed to go below.

"This seems hard treatment," commented Mr. Calvert, "but it is shrewdly suggested by the Egyptian Government officials that the Princess has been sent by Ismail to get up an intrigue against his son Tewfik, with the hope of bringing about his own restoration, which the present government have no intention of permitting. The Princess and party have returned to Italy."

The tension of those days must have tightened nerve and sinew in everyone concerned. It certainly proved too much for Ali Sadik, a colleague of Arabi, who had served as Minister of Finance and had been educated in England. He temporarily lost the balance of his mind under the strain which must have appeared to him as a clash of loyalties. He was reported in *The Times* as having "become insane in consequence of excitement caused by fear of violence from his colleagues".

Throughout May the general situation was most confused. England and France discussed at length what they should do to restore stability, and how and when and if Turkey should be asked to participate. The Khedive was anxious to get Arabi out of power. A deputation from the Chamber expressed their request that the Khedive be reconciled with the Ministers. Arabi warned that if the Ministry was overthrown he could no longer be responsible for public security. England and France replied that if there was any disorder he would find all Europe and Turkey against him, and he would be held responsible.

Finally England and France agreed that they should send an allied squadron to Alexandria. Up to the moment of sailing Lord Granville felt it would have been better to have enlisted the co-operation of more nations in this move, and to have included Turkey. It was not done, however.

The Khedive was to be told of the coming fleet and the Consuls were instructed to advise him that this might be a favourable moment to dismiss the Ministry. But the Consuls replied to their governments that the Khedive would be powerless to form any other unless Arabi's ascendancy was first broken. They therefore contacted the President of the Chamber of Deputies, an erstwhile ally of Arabi who had since decided to withdraw his support. The President was to negotiate with Arabi, with a view to getting him to retire gracefully from his position and from the country. It was hardly surprising that Arabi plainly refused to consider the proposition.

The allied battleships duly arrived and a few days after their appearance the French and English Consuls tried more direct action. They sent an official Note to the President of the Council demanding Arabi's temporary retirement from Egypt. On this the

Ministry did resign, and in doing so they made it quite clear to the Khedive that they considered he had acquiesced in foreign intervention against all the terms by which he was their ruler. They even discussed the possibility of deposing him. Efforts to form another cabinet failed.

None of these moves brought a solution to the situation beyond the flickering hope of a few days, sometimes seemingly to the advantage of one side, sometimes to the other. When France and England, the Khedive, and Arabi's men all reached desperation point (though approaching it from different roads) they came to the conclusion that, after all, the next step might be to ask the Sultan for his opinion. Even so, Egyptian pressure was still put upon the Khedive to end the deadlock by reinstating Arabi in spite of the advice of the Consuls. But he refused.

On 28 May a great gathering took place in Cairo which included the Coptic Patriarch, the Chief Rabbi, and many Professors and learned Sheikhs from Al Azhar. They proceeded to the palace and there requested the Khedive to reinstate Arabi as Minister of War.

According to the official report on the incident, telegraphed from Egypt to the Foreign Office, the above gathering of venerable persons gave a different reason for wishing Arabi's reinstatement than that of nationalist fervour. It was reported that they told the Khedive they had been threatened with death by Arabi if they did not succeed in their mission. It was also thought that the military guard at the Palace had been ordered to prevent the Khedive leaving for his usual drive that day and to fire if he tried to force his way.

It was a time when everyone read into the actions of everyone else the motives which fitted in with their own special conception of the situation. Whatever may have been in the heads of this delegation or in Tewfik's, he yielded to their pressure and Arabi was Minister of War once more. It was at this point that the Khedive formally requested his overlord, the Sultan of Turkey, to send a Commission of Inquiry to Egypt.

CHAPTER VII

TWO DIVIDED COUNTRIES

DURING the spring and early summer of 1882 the train of events in Egypt caused further deep rifts in English public opinion. Wilfrid Blunt, then in England, had some rousing encounters with those who felt differently from himself, he "dined with Rivers Wilson and quarrelled fearfully about Egypt". He took every care in propounding the Egyptian situation when he thought good might come of it. "I met Lady Salisbury who took me aside and cross-questioned me with much appearance of sympathy about the Egyptian cause, and I laid it before her to the best of my ability, knowing that what I said would be repeated to her husband." Blunt visited Mr. Gladstone on purpose to inform him of the civilian leaders of the Egyptian National Party and especially of Sheikh Mohammed Abdu.

Ahmed Arabi was in touch with Mr. Blunt by letter. Much of what he wrote gives food for thought when read today, eight decades later:

"The interests of your English nation. . . in the East, and especially in Egypt, can only be made secure for ever by helping the Egyptians to be free and thus gaining their affection." ". . . As to ourselves also, we thank you for your good services as they concern both Egypt and England, which country we hope will be the most powerful friend to assist us in establishing order on a basis of freedom.

"With regard to the advice you kindly gave us, we have to thank you for it, and beg to say that we are trying our best to keep things quietly and in order, because we consider it one of our most important duties to do so. . . we are with our best will defending the rights of those who dwell in our land, no matter of what nation they may be. All treaties and international obligations are fully respected; and we shall allow no one to touch them as long as the Powers of Europe keep their engagements and friendly relations with us.

"As to the menaces of the great bankers and financial people in Europe, we shall bear them with wisdom and firmness. In our opinion their threats will only hurt themselves and injure those powers who are misled by them."

By early May reports in the London papers spoke of disunity between the civilian and military members of the National party.

Mr. Blunt, in great consternation, sent off eight telegrams to his Egyptian friends, including Arabi, asking if this was true, and stating categorically that if the civilians let themselves be divided from the Army, Europe would annex Egypt. Reassuring answers arrived quickly, which told of unity among themselves and even with the Khedive.

But this cheerful picture did not last long. On the following morning Reuters published, in the London daily papers, the text of Blunt's telegram, and the papers also stated that at least two of the recipients now contradicted the favourable reply they had sent Mr. Blunt in answer to his telegram.

The rash statement that, "Europe will annex you", had, understandably, greatly irritated the British Government. A slight awkwardness followed when an unexpected meeting took place between the Blunts and the Granvilles at a weekend house-party. "His Lordship looked worried," recorded Blunt, "so I auger well for the Nationalists." With other members of the house-party the subject was apparently discussed sympathetically. Mr. Lowell, the American Ambassador, proved to be a strong believer in the National Party.

Almost every social encounter during these weeks resulted in heated debate or icy silence on the question of Egypt. People refused to attend other people's lawn tennis parties till they saw the outcome of events. The elderly Lord Strathairn said that he wished to go out with 10,000 men and hang Arabi. Wilfrid Blunt was called a traitor by his friend Harry Brand who declared that Arabi had made a gigantic fortune and "must and will be suppressed out of Egypt". When a large card arrived for the Blunts from Lady Granville inviting them to the Foreign Office to celebrate Queen Victoria's birthday, Blunt noted in his diary that he would keep it, as an answer to Harry Brand's charge of treason.

In the meantime, Mr. Henry H. Calvert, the Vice-Consul in Alexandria, took up his pen on 6 June to write to his friends, the Rowlatts, in England. This is how the situation appeared to this elderly Englishman viewing it from close quarters:

"Everyone here is on the tiptoe of expectation. . . . Hitherto the military dictator has behaved very arrogantly and with a defiant spirit towards the British and French squadrons.

"Since they have been in harbour he has been engaged in fortifying in a menacing and provocative manner, even throwing up earth-

works and placing guns to fire into the ships. The men-of-war
are of course quite prepared. Their fires are always kept 'banked
up' so as to get up steam at a moment's notice. A day or two ago,
H.M.S. (Ironclad) Monarch arrived and as it was uncertain whether
she would not be fired on, the Admiral (Sir Beauchamp Seymour)
signalled to her to make all speed and to be prepared for action.
So she came in with her big guns ready run out, and in full fighting
trim. But nothing happened. . . .

"So, you see, there is plenty going on from day to day to back
up a sensational state of affairs. Of all the most anxious times we
have recently passed, there has been none to equal the night of Saturday 27th and all Sunday 28th May. The Khedive, on the recom-
mendation of the British and French Consuls-General, cancelled
the appointment of Arabi as Minister of War and Marines. This
news was soon known down here, and caused great excitement
among the troops. . . .

"An 'indignation meeting' took place and the officers telegraphed
back that, if in twelve hours Arabi was not reinstated as Minister,
they would not answer for the consequences, but would not say
what the consequences were likely to be; however, the news oozed
out, that they intended firing on the ships and plundering the
European part of the town, and even bombarding it. You cannot
tell how extreme was the anxiety felt among the Europeans, among
women especially. . . .

"The street, and especially the Square, was filled with people
full of apprehension. Few went to bed that night, or those who did,
had not much sleep. I know that, what with writing and ciphering
for several hours at night, my brain was excited, and I only slept
at daybreak. All night long I heard carriages passing to and fro
between Ras al Tin and Rosetta Gate, full of Egyptian officers,
who were probably maturing their plans. However, much of the
alarm subsided on the Khedive promising to retain Arabi in office
for the present, he guaranteeing the public security.

"Of course, neither England nor France, nor probably Turkey
will permit of the bold soldier braving all authority much longer.
You, perhaps, know that he aspires to the throne of Egypt and has
compelled thousands of natives to sign a petition to the Sultan in
his favour, of course this being done under compulsion. . . .

"People go anywhere, so long as they can get away—to Syria,
Smyrna, Constantinople, Greece, Cyprus, Italy, France, Malta—

it little matters. All financial Israel has left taking all their money with them. The steamers are crowded. Even well-to-do persons take deck passages. Some people are so thoroughly demoralised by fright that they purchase tickets at a very high figure. The exodus of Maltese is immense. It is as much as one of our clerks can do to give the people their passports. . . .

"The natives are beginning to feel the effect of the crises. Many are taken away from their fields, when their presence is much required, and cultivators cannot obtain advances on crops. People building houses have suspended operations, not knowing what may happen. Shopkeepers have desired their agents in Europe to keep back goods. In a word, if this crisis lasts, great misery will be the result.

"As far as one can judge, Arabi is feared but not liked, except by the army and a few fanatics. The native population do not show any hostility towards the Europeans, and nothing reveals the possibility of troublous times in this City. I do not think there will be any danger run by the European population, if there were, surely Italian, Russian, Austrian, and other vessels of war would come here to protect their subjects; but none have come.

"It strikes me that this valiant army and active population have more fear of us than we of them.

"The Governor asked the Greek Consul whether it was true that 3,000 Greeks had been supplied with arms, and if so, how they obtained them. The Consul confirmed these rumours, but probably he did so to let the Egyptians know that every one is ready. In fact all the Europeans, whatever their nationality, are bound together for their mutual defence.

"The Italian and French operatives promise a strong contingent, and if fighting does take place, barricades will be run up in the streets to keep the soldiers out of the European quarter. . . . "

In the meantime Constantinople had received Khedive Tewfik's request for an official enquiry which resulted in Darwish Pasha being sent as Commissioner for the Sultan of Turkey. He duly arrived on the 7 June aboard the Turkish yacht Izedin, accompanied by various notables, a whole suite of secretaries and 25 military staff officers. With him also came Essad Effendi, described as "le Lieutenant de la garde du tombeau du Prophete",[1] who was a fellow

---

[1] See *l'Egypte Contemporaire et Arabi Pasha* by N. Scotides, Paris, 1888, p. 83.

Commissioner. In their baggage were packed 200 noble orders to be dispensed on behalf of the Sultan, as strategy dictated, to left or to right. Both Arabi and the Khedive sent their representatives to greet them, and the European Consuls and the French and English Admirals also called to pay their respects.

After a stay of only a few hours at the Ras al Tin Palace, Darwish and Essad moved off to Cairo where they took up their residence at the Gezira Palace. In both towns they were given a warm reception by the crowds who ran beside the carriages shouting war cries, variously reported as "God, give victory to the Sultan"; "Send away the fleet"; "Reject the ultimatum"; "Long live Islam, long live the Prophet"; "Down with the Christians, the dogs of Christians". There was probably some lad at some time in the proceedings, shouting each of them.

Darwish Pasha's past would have made a horror film to delight any cinema box office. As a military general he had been sent to reduce rebel Montenegrins to order; slaughter, torture and deceit were the methods. His means of extortion in Albania were imaginative and refined. An article in the *Pall Mall Gazette* of 15 June 1882, by John Morley, comments thus on Darwish's visit to Egypt: "Nothing can be more striking than his assertion of authority, and nothing more skilful than his casual reference to the massacre of the Mamelukes. Darwish is a man of iron, and Arabi may well quail before his eye. One saucy word and his head would roll upon the carpet. Darwish is quite capable of 'manipulating' Arabi, not in the Western but in the Eastern sense of the word. In this strong resolute Ottoman it seems probable that the revolution in Egypt has found its master."

He refused at first to see Arabi, but he received various Sheikhs of Al Azhar some of whom spoke plainly about their support of Arabi and suggested that the Commissioner might well join them in this support.

Darwish Pasha, however, did not take kindly to this suggestion and answered that he had not come to Egypt to receive orders but to give them. To add point to his answer his large-sized attendant, who was always to hand, forcibly removed the Sheikh who had addressed the Pasha thus. The Sheikhs were furious at this treatment and a meeting of protest was held by the students at Al Azhar mosque on the following day at which comment was freely made.

The role of Essad Effendi, as fellow Commissioner, was most

peculiar. Authors with such opposite views as Lord Cromer and Mr. Blunt agree that the Sultan had thought fit to issue both Commissioners with secret orders, one lot being a contradiction of the other. Darwish was to co-operate with the Khedive and Essad with Arabi. Both men were given a different code with which to communicate with the Sultan.

On 10 June Darwish received Arabi in private audience. He was courteous in his manner but Arabi noticed that Darwish offered him no coffee. The old Turk opened the conversation in a man to man fashion, agreeing how tiresome was the presence of the European naval squadrons, and how just were Arabi's grievances. The Sultan, he affirmed, wanted nothing better than good understanding with his dear Egyptian family. Slowly he came to the point—Arabi was to hand over the command of affairs to himself, Darwish, while Arabi was to take the heaven-sent opportunity of visiting Constantinople there to gather the ineffable advantage of talking things over with their August Master himself.

Arabi could not have failed to see this trap. He had assuredly known of more people going to Constantinople on such missions than he had ever known to return. But he parried the point by falling in with the idea, on one condition. It was that he should get a total discharge of administration of affairs in the names of the Sultan, the Khedive and Darwish; and that he should also be relieved of his undertaking, solemnly given to the European Consuls in Egypt, that the country would be tranquil while he was at his post. That being the case Arabi expressed himself as ready to go. But Darwish was not ready—not under those conditions—though he naturally did not show it. "Good, that is understood," he said as he bowed his visitors out, "I am your successor and you will go to Constantinople before me." Little more was heard from him on that line, however.[2]

Arabi's interview with Darwish took place on June 10th, 1882. On the next day, serious riots broke out in Alexandria. By this time, my grandfather, J. E. Cornish, was managing director of the Alexandria Water Company and was present throughout these events. That evening he and my grandmother drove some friends to the railway station. Having previously heard that there had

[2] For the above information, see *Arabi Pasha* by J. Ninet, 1884, p.95. Privately printed in French, St. Quentin, Imprimerie J. Moureau et Fils, and Sir Edward Malet's official report on the incident.

been a riot in the town and several people had been killed, they decided to take a circuitous route thus avoiding the central part of the town. They remarked that not a single carriage came from the town for the express train to Cairo and they could hear a noise ("as of a considerable row", said my grandfather) coming from the centre of the town.

On their return journey a crowd met them running towards the town, armed with sticks; a street carriage which followed was stoned and they afterwards heard that its occupants had been hurt. They themselves received nothing worse than abuse.

At one point, some men came out into the road, as if to stop the carriage, but the Cornishes were recognised by some of them who called the others back. On reaching home they were alarmed to find that the governess had gone for a walk with two of their children and had not returned. They immediately went in search of them. They were soon found, quite safe, but the governess said they had been frightened by Bedouin who had hooted at and threatened them. The two children were probably my uncle, the future managing director of the Alexandria Water Company, and my mother, aged seven and five. I much doubt if this incident caused them anything but relish in spite of what the governess might have felt.

News soon reached the Cornishes that a large number of Europeans were killed and that all the English were ordered to go to the Consulate for safety. This order had an immediate effect on my grandfather. He decided that his family would remain where they were. He began to see what arms he could muster, but only found an old pistol and two cartridges. The chief mechanic said he had a gun, but on going to fetch it, found he had lent it to a friend in the town. Early next morning Cornish showed the few men who came to the workshop how to make hand-pikes with steel heads. He then drove to the armourer's shops in the town to buy weapons and ammunition, if possible.

He was stopped at the town gate by soldiers, who searched him for a pistol; he had nothing but a walking stick which was taken away. The armourers' shops were guarded by soldiers who kept the people off. My grandfather's concern was to keep Alexandria supplied with water so he went to Omar Pasha Loutfi, the Governor of the town, and explained the position. The Water Works had a cargo of coal in the port, and all arrangements were made for carting it to the works in the morning. But if it did not arrive then there

احمد عرابي المصري

Ahmed Arabi, from a sketch by Frederick Villiers,
Special Correspondent of *The Graphic* in Egypt, 1882.

Sheikh Mohammed Abdu taken on the terrace of the House
of Commons, London, 22 May, 1844.
(Reproduced by permission of the Syndics of the Fitwilliam
Museum, Cambridge, England.)

The Bank of Egypt, Alexandria, after the Bombardment and fire, 1882. (From an original photograph in the author's possession.)

Ahmed Arabi receiving a dispatch: as seen by the
artist of *The London Illustrated News*, Published
July 22, 1882.

Tents of the British Army at Ramleh, outside Alexandria, 1882. (From an original photograph in the possession of the author.)

Alexandria buildings after the bombardment and fire, 1882. (From an original photograph in the author's possession.)

Trial of Arabi Pasha before the Egyptian Court-Martial at Cairo.
(Published in *The Illustrated London News*, December 23, 1882.)
1. Arabi Pasha 2. Mr. Broadley, Counsel for prisoner.

Mr. Cornish, managing Director of the Alexandria Water
Works, photographed with his family in their garden at
Alexandria. His daughter in the sailor-suit is now Lady
Rowlatt, the author's mother.

The war in Egypt: The guards as equipped for service in Egypt. This equipment included dark glasses and veils against sun and sand. (Published in *The London Illustrated News*, August 12, 1882.)

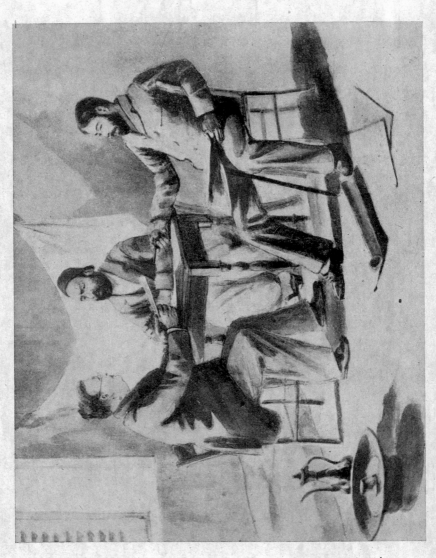

Ahmed Arabi in his cell, with
Mr. Broadley and Mr. Napier
1882. (From a sketch by Frederick
Villiers, Special correspondent of
The Graphic in Egypt.)

was only enough coal at the pumping station to keep it working for about fifteen hours.

The Governor at once saw that it was a serious matter in view of the already excited state of the town. He had been up all night in imminent danger of his life, he was anxious and busy, giving many orders referring to the safety of different parts of the town, but he calmly discussed with Cornish the best steps to be taken. The Governor sent a delegate with my grandfather and a letter to the Chief of the Customs, to render every assistance in his power.[3]

At the Custom House they could not find a single official capable either of reading the letter or writing the order to the men in charge of the locks to let the coal lighters pass into the Canal. This was the only way of getting the coal, for there were no dock labourers on the quays, and no carts could be found. Cornish decided to try at other locks; but to get there they would have had to pass the site of the massacre, and the Governor's delegate came to the conclusion that he was too busy. He was told that if he did not go he would be driven back to the Governor, and another man asked for, with more time on his hands. His mind battled between two evils, and at length he chose the lesser and accompanied Cornish.

On arriving at the locks they found a few men loafing about, but were told that the Chief was a little indisposed, and might not come that day. They said that it would be impossible to pass any barges through, because there was no one to write the necessary order, but after a while they became convinced of the possibility, if they were paid £2 down, and £3 more when two barges had got half way. During this discussion the delegate disappeared, nor was he seen again.

With much difficulty a boat was induced to go off to the coal ship; then a soldier on the quay threatened to shoot the boatman if he did so and much further time was lost before he was persuaded otherwise. On board the collier, my grandfather found the Captain and crew in an uncomfortable frame of mind. Three of the crew had been in the troubles of the previous day, all were hurt, the mate had his arm broken and his head covered with bandages, the cook had disappeared altogether, and they thought he was killed. It took nearly all that day and most of the next night for Cornish

[3] Some authorities believe that contrary to the impression my grandfather received, Omar Loutfi was more responsible than any one else for the riots. See *Egypt*, Tom Little, Benn, 1958, p. 88.

to get coal up to the pumping station, just in time to keep the machinery going.

What actually set in motion the massacre of 11 June will probably never be known; opinions of the time and opinions of today vary on the point. But what was certain and what mattered, was that all necessary conditions for spontaneous combustion were present, high-hand demeanour and under-hand deceit. A story in general circulation was that a Maltese (or Greek) had hired a carriage (or donkey) and driven to a café (or grocer's shop) after which he had refused to pay the coachman (or donkey boy) who had thereupon killed (or wounded) the Maltese (or Greek). Some enterprising writers of the time, dotted i's and crossed t's, thus the European had actually been the British Consul-General's valet's brother and the weapon used to kill him had actually been a cheese knife attached by a piece of string to the cheese.

Some people denied that any unforeseen quarrel had started it off. One English resident who took refuge in Cyprus wrote: "I am fully of the opinion that the riot of the 11th was the issue of a pre-concerted plan concocted by Arabi Pasha and his partisans; I may state that I was warned by a friend, that the riot would break out on Sunday, the 11th, but I am convinced that it took place 3 hours sooner than was intended, and consequently it did not assume such serious proportions as were designed or hoped for by those who were responsible for it.

"The story of a dispute between a Maltese (or a Greek) and an Arab donkey-boy is, I consider, simply a screen, wretchedly constructed, as a 'blind' and unworthy of my consideration. . . ."

The British Government requested further statements from a number of English and other refugees. A well-known English resident spoke of, "Little indications which one did not pay attention to at the time, such as, on Saturday morning, when leaving my house, a vegetable-seller in the street told me to buy and eat now, as tomorrow the Christians would be massacred. These words I found afterwards were said to a great many people, who paid little or no attention to them. . . ."[4]

Volumes have been filled on the subject of who was to blame for these events, and an equal number of volumes on who was not to blame, but little has been proven, for the people on whom the blame was pinned in one set of volumes, were the same people

---

[4] For these two statements see Parliamentary Papers, Egypt, No. 16, 1882.

from whom the blame was removed in the other set of volumes.
Ergo? But the fact remained, the "noise as of a considerable row"
to which my grandfather alluded, was produced by scenes of real
carnage in which the streets were littered with dead and dying Europeans and Egyptians.

Mr. Cookson, the British Consul, was wounded in the head by
stones and heavy sticks; according to a Greek reporter, he would
undoubtedly have been killed had not an Egyptian Sheikh protected
him from his assailants. This same Greek, Mr. Scotides, tells
how many Europeans were visiting the allied men-of-war and
unaware of the state of the town, were returning to it in boats
when they were killed with the oars of the boatmen. The English
and French admirals had a narrow escape while trying to get from
the town back to their ship, but they were greatly helped by an
Egyptian officer who used his sword mightily to keep off the crowds.
The French admiral, having escaped the mob, was nearly squashed
between the two heavy dockyard doors which were closed behind
them for final safety.

Another eye-witness is worth mentioning, partly because the book
he wrote of his experiences is now extremely rare, and partly because he throws light on the atmosphere which engendered the
events even if he does not add much to our knowledge of the events
themselves. The writer was an elderly Swiss, called Jean Ninet.
He was known to my grandfather who met him in the spring of 1881
at a luncheon party given by a British resident of Alexandria in
honour of the Duke of Sutherland. Ninet originally came to Egypt
as an authority on cotton in the time of Mohammed Ali; he later
became a close friend and supporter of Arabi. J. E. Cornish admired
Ninet's writings on the cultivation of cotton but was somewhat
scathing about his political outlook on Egyptian affairs.

On 10 June 1882 (the eve of the riots) Jean Ninet attended an
assembly of Egyptian notables in Alexandria. The speeches delivered on this occasion were highly charged with passion. Ninet,
whose Arabic was fluent, noted down the points, as he heard them.
One particularly good orator swept his audience with him as he
underlined his view that the British fleet, riding at anchor outside
the town as he spoke, was armed and was therefore an enemy
and desirous of mastering Egypt, not befriending her. The speaker
dealt with Darwish peremptorily by saying that his words were
empty and his power to help them was nil, for he had already been

heavily bribed by the Sultan. This was not the view of the speaker alone, for it was widely recounted at the time that Darwish had received £40,000, promising to share it with others, which, in fact, he had not done. But two of his subordinates, so it was rumoured, had sold the Sultan's cipher key to the Khedive, thus doing well for themselves also.[5]

This Egyptian speaker then gave his ideas about what was going on in the minds of the English admiral and sailors as they watched Alexandria from their vessels. In spite of the fact that these Englishmen take the Egyptians for dogs, he explained, yet they know that their mission is unjust towards Egypt; an inner voice tells them that Egyptians, as well as themselves, have a heart capable of feeling gratuitous insults from anyone, but above all from foreigners.

The speech ended with a call for unity, so that, when the moment came the Egyptians could take effective action.

The sad news of the events of 11 June did not reach Arabi in Cairo till about 5 p.m. He immediately ordered the Colonels in Alexandria to use their troops to restore order. By the evening quiet reigned over the blood-stained city. On the next day Arabi issued the following order:

"Today a superior order has come to me, from His Highness the Khedive. This order says that the Consuls-General having been to His Highness, spoke with him about the situation, in the presence of His Excellency Darwish Pasha, and requested him that the lives and goods of their nationals living in Egypt might be guaranteed.

"His Highness acquiesced to this demand and has guaranteed the life and goods of foreign administrators knowing that the Egyptian Army is fulfilling, and always will fulfil, its duties, duties which include the maintenance of order and public security. . . .

"The superior order also says that, just as I am held personally responsible to His Highness, so each officer will be held responsible to me. It is your duty to take the most efficacious measures to appease the over-excitement and to ensure tranquillity.

"Be carefully watchful over the population, whether native or foreign, and take for the basis of your conduct civil morality and the duties which every good citizen, animated by love of his country and its prosperity, should constantly follow."

Notwithstanding, the spirit of confidence did not return. She

[5] See *Egypt and the Egyptian Question* by D. Mackenzie Wallace, Macmillan, 1883, p. 86.

was by then but a nebulous, emaciated ghost of confidence to which no edict could give life. The European communities streamed away in constant flow, thus forcing the refugee problem to be faced squarely. It was soon officially realised that not only immediate help was needed but aid to re-start life for many who had been ruined.[6]

The Lord Mayor of London opened a relief fund to which Lord Granville was the first to subscribe, with £100. Further reminders followed. "The organisation for the relief and accommodation of indigent English refugees is worthy of notice. . . . These 3,319 refugees averaging 664 in each vessel, have been in the hands of the organisation for periods averaging, perhaps 20 days for each person. The vessels employed have been colliers, utterly unprepared to meet the occasion. . . . It must be remembered that England is considered largely responsible for the present state of things in Egypt. . . . The majority of these consist of. . . Maltese, huddled up together in the hold, with suddenly extemporised sanitary arrangements. They range through all ages, from the baby newly born on board, to the patriarch of 92" (*The Times*, 7 July 1882).

Three days later the harassed Lord Mayor received a cable from the Governor and Commander-in-Chief at Malta, General Sir Arthur Borton:

"The £1,000 remittance exhausted. The total number of refugees arrived 7,800 but a telegram from Admiral Sir Beauchamp Seymour states that 445 more left Alexandria yesterday, making a grand total of 8,245. The present expenditure is £84 daily, but it is likely to rise to £150 per day. The resources of the island are totally inadequate to meet such outlay. Further funds are urgently required."

Feeling was running high in England during these days. A circular addressed to members of the Anti-Aggression League was widely published. It is a masterful pronouncement more prophetic in general principle than its authors probably realised. "A powerful English fleet is drawn up in battle array before the armed batteries of the port of Alexandria. . .under the guns of the ships the English envoys have been demanding the dismissal of a native Ministry. Already disaster is upon us and further disaster is to be feared. The obvious cause of the disorder in Egypt is a system of vexatious interference in the internal government of the country and the attempt to dictate its Ministries and to direct its politics. . . .

[6] See letter from Sir Edward Malet to Lord Granville, *The Times*, 21 June 1882.

"It is not the duty of private citizens either to administer foreign affairs or to dictate diplomatic expedients. Their duty, however, is plain—to insist that the Government should not drag the nation to the verge of war and embroil it with a foreign people without adequate cause. Protection of British interests is the general purpose alleged. What British interests? We quite recognise the interest which Great Britain has in securing the use of the Suez Canal as an open waterway, but this interest is not endangered. Maintenance of it is not even mentioned among the ends above enumerated as necessitating action.

"The sole British interest specified by the Prime Minister is that of the bondholders. . . . If, that Egypt may be so administered that it can pay its debts, we are to maintain on its throne our nominee, agent, or middle-man, then, for indefinite periods, a British fleet will have to parade before the ports of Alexandria every time that a Khedive of our choosing happens to find himself in a Ministerial crisis at Cairo. To keep this or that Prince permanently on the throne, to maintain by force a stereotyped Government in Cairo, is a task too great for ingenious protocols, with or without ironclads at Alexandria. It means the practical assumption of the government of a considerable nation. The exercise of such authority implies the imminent risk of a European war. . .vague possibilities of damage in no way satisfy us, for they can be plausibly discovered in every possible situation. . . . To ward off possible evils we have brought on ourselves actual disasters.

"If it be alleged that the course taken be imperative because, if we were to leave Egypt to itself, some other European Power would gain predominance, and our free use of the Canal would be endangered, then the reply is that a policy far less dangerous than the present one, would be that of abstaining from interference ourselves on the understanding that no other Power should interfere. A European concert on this basis would commend itself to all concerned. Leaving undiscussed the question whether the present Administration could, in view of engagements made by their predecessors, have done otherwise than they have done, we may fitly urge that these engagements should be brought to a close as quickly as possible, and may wisely prepare ourselves to protest in future cases against the meddling policy which entails these entanglements."

CHAPTER VIII

THE SKY DARKENS

As members of the British public were expressing their feelings the actual scene in Alexandria was fast unrolling.

My grandfather Cornish called on the Egyptian Prime Minister requesting that a guard of ten horse soldiers with an officer should be stationed outside the Waterworks gates, and that a guard of four soldiers should accompany him wherever he wanted to go. This request was first granted but later refused as being unnecessary. My grandfather describes the scene from the windows of Ras al Tin Palace where he had been sitting on this occasion for more than three hours: "I could see the harbour crowded with boats taking off hundreds of Europeans to scores of steamers most of which appeared already crowded. Some official kindly supplied me with a telescope which enabled me to notice that most of the people in the boats seemed to be quarrelling, and as far as I could make out, the boatmen were taking them anywhere except direct to their ships, probably until they had extracted from these unfortunate people the last piastre they could get. I afterwards heard that many were thrown overboard in the struggle; it looked like a regular 'sauve qui peut' and that they thought something unpleasant would happen to the hindermost."

Soon after this, Cornish saw Arabi himself who assured him that special orders had been given for his protection, and that he might go where he would without fear. He did not feel satisfied, however, and began seriously making the best arrangements he could for the defence of the premises. They fortunately had a considerable quantity of electric lighting material, the first ever brought to Egypt, which proved useful. The principal engine room was walled up except for one small door, and the upper windows were fitted with loop holes.

A blow-off pipe from the boilers was laid just outside the only door and was capable of discharging a large quantity of steam and boiling water. The staircase leading to the upper floor was taken away and replaced by a light removable ladder; an electric cable was laid round the building and its approaches. Ten large bombs connected to batteries and the electric touches in the engine room, could be exploded by anyone seeing the surroundings without being observed. The British Admiral had supplied fulminate of mercury fuzes and other appliances for making these bombs, and had allowed one of his torpedo officers to assist in preparing them. Cornish had with some difficulty succeeded in getting 17 guns, as many revolvers, and a good supply of ammunition, some of which had been given by friends leaving the country, and a good supply of dynamite hand-grenades was found among the household goods of an employee who had run away.

Thus prepared in case of emergency my grandfather did not hesitate to enter the town, though some of his visits might not be deemed absolutely necessary. One day he decided that it would be a good idea to paint a gold streak round the tender of his launch to smarten her up for whatever adventures lay ahead. He went to the shop of a French colourman and found him in an agitated state preparing to leave. When asked for gilding he thought he was faced with an English madman. Other journeys to the town bore more relation to circumstances.

On the morning of 1 July a report had been started that the English had poisoned the water supply, and criers were sent about warning the people not to drink any water from the taps. Cornish had been up all night superintending some repairs in the town and only returned home about 7 a.m. so had heard nothing of the rumour. He drove into the town again, about ten, and was surprised to find his carriage stopped several times by a crowd, and himself nearly dragged out of it. He discovered eventually what was the supposed trouble, but even so, had it not been for his trustworthy policeman who laid about him with a heavy stick he would have come off badly.

On another day when Cornish was absent, Arabi accompanied by the Prime Minister and a large staff, visited the Waterworks and questioned several of the workmen. Arabi himself climbed to the engine loft and examined it minutely. He saw several hundred bottles filled with filtered water which he had been told contained poison. He insisted on the chief mechanic drinking from several of them, and as this was done without hesitation, he tasted the water himself and told his followers that all was well. He noticed a closed cabinet which contained the electric touches for exploding the bombs, this was locked but Arabi had it broken open and touched some of the buttons. His friends below in the courtyard were sitting within a few feet of two of the bombs, but fortunately for them, the branch wires were not yet connected to the main cable. Arabi had some trenches dug in the yard and found the cable, but the Waterworks staff persuaded him that the whole arrangement was for electric lighting. Before leaving, Arabi told his friends that there did not appear to be any offensive arrangements and he thought no harm would come from that quarter if it were left alone; the party then left. Cornish arrived at the works a few minutes after and was told of this incident.

Cornish kept in close touch with Admiral Sir Beauchamp Seymour in command of the British squadron, and he paid frequent visits to the flag ship. One day, while waiting for the Admiral to appear, he took a look at the chart spread out on a table, marking the positions of the different ships and their lines of fire. He seized a pencil and clearly indicated on this chart the exact position of the Waterworks. The Admiral promised to instruct his captains to do their best to avoid that spot in the event of bombing as there would be an Englishman there.

Quarters had been reserved for my grandfather in the Monarch and he was again urged to take refuge afloat as virtually all the European communities had done. But he was firm on the point, though he had mercifully decided to evacuate his wife and five children who were already on a boat bound for Beirut. As Mr. Auckland Colvin left Alexandria he gave my grandfather till ten next morning 9 July in which to change his mind, for an imminent bombardment was now taken for granted. His mind was made up, however, and he declined to leave.

As Cornish said goodbye to some friends on a P. & O. refugee ship, before his final trip back to Alexandria across the harbour, one man was heard saying to another: "Poor fellow, that is most likely the last we shall see of him."

He passed all the large men-of-war outside the breakwater. They had their top masts struck, all possible rigging hauled down, and decks apparently cleared for action, presenting altogether a very formidable and ominous appearance. "In the distance the town looked as quiet and peaceable as possible," he wrote of the scene, "the sun lit up some of the more distant minarets, and it seemed sad to think what a work of destruction was to begin the next morning. Just as we entered the inner harbour, we passed the last man-of-war leaving it, a very handsome wooden frigate, the Austrian[1] flag ship—she was playing the national anthem, and we dipped our British ensign in salute, which the ship graciously returned. Some officer on the quarter deck shouted at us, probably to ask what we meant by running inshore at such a time."

My grandfather's launch had a crew of four, and on arrival at the breakwater he gave them the choice of landing with him or staying afloat in the launch which had ample provisions. They chose the latter and there they stayed safely under the breakwater throughout the bombardment. "I must own that I left with some reluctance," was Cornish's comment. He found the port gates closed and in charge of two black men who fortunately knew him. They at first refused to open, saying "Go back to a ship, this is no place for Franghis [Europeans] now". But when they had agreed about the amount required to calm their scruples, they let him pass. He decided to go through the Rosetta Gate where he was better known to the soldiers, for he dreaded being stopped in the town.

Progress was not easy, for the local inhabitants had come to the conclusion that a bombardment would take place and were crowding out of Alexandria, some making for canal boats, some for the railway and some just out into the open hardly knowing what to do for the best. Carts and barrows loaded with women, children and furniture kept the sad procession at a funeral pace. "There was no getting away from them," wrote my grandfather, "and the sight of a European seemed to get on their nerves"— possibly an understatement.

When he eventually reached the Waterworks safely he reviewed the position and concluded that he and the few workmen left could resist anything short of a large scale serious attack by Arabi's troops. He had secured a stock of flour, rice and biscuits, ten live sheep, about 300 head of poultry, and had a baker and an oven. "I thanked God that we were better off than we might have been," he said, "and being very tired I slept soundly until five next morning."

Old Jean Ninet, the Swiss, was also on the scene these days. He eyed the British admiral from the shore with mistrust, describing him as appearing on deck each dawn dressed in a jersey, his bare feet emerging from "large pantalon de matin", as he scanned Arabi's fortifications with an eye to attacking them. Ninet rides his imagina-

[1] Other nations had sent warships to stand by in the crisis but all except England finally decided to take no part in the coming events.

tion on a loose rein when he accuses the admiral of playing "au Jupiter tonnant et jurant du matin au soir".

A study of the Parliamentary Papers of the day shows that Admiral Seymour was not acting the thundering Jupiter all day for he was much concerned with the great exodus of refugees. His despatch to the Secretary of the Admiralty of 27 June dwells on it: "In the case of the Rhosina which sailed today at 11 a.m. we have had to fit her up from our own resources as best we may, and I have been obliged to procure the services of a medical practitioner to proceed to Malta in her, at the high rate of pay of £60 for the voyage, in consequence of the number of ladies and women on board who are daily expecting their confinement." Latona was more his role, on occasions, than Jupiter.

Ninet's description of his own movements during the day of the massacre have a ring of truth about them, however. In front of St. Mark's buildings he passes a French Marquis, "running as fast as his little legs would carry him, to his home. 'What are you doing here? They are murdering over there,' he cried at me. And he disappeared." Ninet went up Rue Sherif Pasha to try and console an Anglo-Italian family whom he knew, composed mostly of ladies, the one man being ill and unable to move. A strong negro armed with a big stick flourished it and followed him. "What are you up to? I have not harmed you," said Ninet, "I am the doctor come to see the sick man." On this he was let in. As he left the house he met an Egyptian infantry officer of his acquaintance, who addressed him: "Brother, take cover, the soldiers are beginning. Arabi has just sent the necessary orders."

Colonel Chaillé Long, the American, was also on the scene. He tells of the sudden departure of the acting consular agent of the United States who was an Austrian subject though Levantine by race. Members of the American community in vain requested him not to desert his post, but his answer, according to Colonel Chaillé Long, was brief and to the point. "My personal safety is of more importance to me than the office of consular agent which costs me a great deal of money." Whereupon the Colonel himself became the United States Consul.

The official American attitude to the situation was stated with a clarity which left no room for doubtful interpretation. A despatch from Philadelphia, on 6 July read: "The United States Government will take no part in the Egyptian conflict beyond protecting American

residents in Egypt, who are, however, so few that they may readily
be received on board of the four American naval vessels now in
Egyptian waters. American policy forbids any interference in
European complications."

On 4 July the Americans nearly caused a complication themselves.
Their Admiral announced his intention of firing a salvo of guns in
commemoration of American independence. When the Khedive
heard of this he sent his Master of Ceremonies to ask if it could be
foregone in view of the highly-strung condition of the populace.
But it was explained to the Court Official that the 4th of July was
the American "Bairam", and that the Admiral could not consider
cancelling his salute. "No, sir! I shall do nothing of the kind.
Whoever heard of such a thing?" said he to the intermediary,
Colonel Long.

(It may be noted that, in spite of America's wish not to be involved,
on 15 July a British consular despatch to the Foreign Office included
the comment, "Native police are being organised to work with
American Marines.")

As the American ships steamed off with their quota of refugees,
they saluted the British men-of-war and their band played "God
save the Queen" which was answered by the Englishmen with "Hail
Columbia".

Colonel Chaillé Long gives a lively picture of the janissary, Ali,
attached to the American consulate, dressed in his highly coloured
and gold-laced Turkish costume, as such men in the employ of
present legations and embassies still wear. "Ali", he writes, "was
a pious (?) Mohammedan, but, in defiance of his faith, never refused
ardent spirits. Twenty five years service in the American consulate
had gotten him over that prejudice. Ali was a born diplomat,
and I delighted at night to engage him in conversation about Arabi.
'Your Excellency,' said he, 'the work of Arabi is the work of the
devil. By Allah, it is true.' " The old hired coachman who drove
Colonel Long, spoke to him thus of Arabi, "O Bey, Arabi is a fool
(magnoon). He has driven out the Europeans. What shall we
do with our carriages? It is not the fellah who will ride in them.
We shall starve!"

In the meantime, great diplomatic activity reverberated between
London and Paris, where de Fréycinet was now the Foreign Minister
in place of Gambetta. On 5 July Lord Lyons, the British Ambassador
in Paris, reported to the Foreign Office that the French Govern-

ment could not instruct their admiral to associate himself with the English admiral in stopping by force the erection of batteries or the placing of guns at Alexandria, as they "considered that this would be an act of offensive hostility against Egypt in which they could not take part without violating the Constitution which prohibits their making war without the consent of the Chambers".[2]

This occasioned some feeling between the two countries. The views of an anonymous Frenchman were reported in *The Times* of 7 July for all to read:

"The English. . .have the faults attached to their good qualities. They are more unbending, inaccessible and exclusive. They always and everywhere live, as it were, on an island. They walk together, eat together, play at lawn tennis together. They are always foreigners, and always look upon others, even the inhabitants of the country they are in as foreigners. The result of this is that their policy is never a policy of compromise; it is an absolute all or nothing policy—always personified in somebody—Yakoob, Cetywayo, or Arabi.

"Hence no understanding is possible, and somebody has to be exterminated in order to solve the question. It is just now Arabi, because the English policy has been such that the honour of England is pledged to Arabi's disappearance from the scene. . . .

"I once had an intimate friend who was possessed with a craving to commit suicide. I passed months in dissuading him from it. One day, when crossing the Solferino bridge with him, he sprang over the parapet into the river. I did not follow him, therefore I was not fortunate enough to save him. Ought I to have jumped over after him? I do not say that England could commit suicide about Egypt. No, indeed; I am aware that she swims well. But if only to avoid a chill it is better not to jump over parapets, without being forced to do so. Well, at this moment England wishes to jump over a parapet, and my opinion is that she might avoid any necessity of it."

In the meantime, Darwish Pasha, the Sultan's Envoy sent to unravel this tangle, must have been feeling his years. He did not lay about him with the blood and thunder predicted earlier by the *Pall Mall Gazette*. On 2 July he issued a proclamation which had as much

[2] State Papers, 1882-83, Vol. 74, p. 480.

influence on the people to whom it was addressed, as the summer breeze that blew around them.

"I hereby give notice to all the natives of Egypt and those residing in, or resorting to, Egypt, that I, the Special Envoy of the High Caliph in the two lands and of the Commander of the Faithful, our most exalted Lord the Sultan, who has always at heart the welfare of his States and is unwilling to allow any infringement of his Imperial Orders granting privileges to the Khedive, do hereby enjoin upon the natives to be obedient to the commands of the Most High (obey God, His Prophet and those who are in authority). . . . It has been the gracious will of His Exalted Majesty to send me with the other Commissioners to Egypt, to enforce obedience to His Highness the Khedive by high and low without distinction of creed or nationality, and who ever may disobey the above orders will be an outcast from society and will have incurred His Majesty's displeasure.

". . .This is for the information of the public and for all persons, in order that they may continue to enjoy peace and tranquillity under the shadow of the High Caliph, and attend to their own business without occupying themselves with matters that do not concern them.

"Prosperity is derived from commerce, and commerce is assured by public security. I caution all persons, whether native or foreigners, to act in accordance with the above instructions, to live in brotherly harmony and to observe the principles of civilized intercourse."

Sheikh Mohammed Abdu must have been among the many who read this. It may be imagined that in doing so his mind went back to his old great-uncle of the same name—Darwish—but of so different a character. Whatever the effect of this edict on Mohammed Abdu, its effect on Arabi can be judged by the following telegram sent to the Minister of Foreign Affairs in London by the British Ambassador in Constantinople:

"I have the honour to inform your Lordship that the Sublime Porte has been informed that Arabi Pasha has intimated to Darwish Pasha that he had better quit Egypt."[3]

On 7 July Admiral Seymour informed the Egyptian Military Commandant that, as it had been reported to him that two more guns were being mounted on the sea defences, it would be his duty

[3] For the above information see Parliamentary Papers, Egypt, No. 17.

to open fire on the works unless they were immediately stopped.

This was followed in a few days by a further ultimatum stating that unless there was a temporary surrender of the forts for the purpose of disarmament the British ships would open fire in twenty-four hours.

A hurried meeting took place at the Palace of Ras al Tin on the receipt of this communication. The Khedive presided, Darwish Pasha was there, and of course Arabi, as Minister of War. An answering letter was drafted and sent to the Admiral.

"Sir, Egypt has done nothing to warrant the sending of the assembled Allied squadron of battleships before Alexandria. The authorities, both civil and military, have likewise done nothing to justify the ultimatum sent by the admiral. The forts are in the same state as they were when the squadron entered the port with the exception of some urgent repairs that had to be made in some old forts, but, sir, we are here in our land and homes and it is our right, nay, our duty to take measure against all enemies who want to take us by surprise and disturb our peaceful relations—those relations which the English Government profess to maintain with us. Egypt, true to her rights and her honour, cannot without coercion yield any of her batteries or guns.

"She protests against your ultimatum of this morning and leaves the responsibility, of having opened fire, to fall on the head of the nation that fires the first shell at Alexandria, this peaceful city, thus contravening the laws of war and of humanity."[4]

Sir Beauchamp Seymour kept the Admiralty informed of proceedings by a series of detailed despatches.

"I have the honour to request that you will acquaint the Lords Commissioners of the Admiralty that. . .

"Having failed to obtain compliance with the demands which I was directed to make on the 'de facto' rulers of Egypt, I attacked the batteries. . . . and succeeded in silencing the forts at 5.30 p.m. . . .

"On the morning of the 12th I ordered the Temeraire and Inflexible to engage Fort Pharos, unfortunately this meant the destruction of a beautiful 15th century mosque which stood within the fort. . . .

"I regret to say that the city of Alexandria has suffered greatly by fire and pillage. . . .

"The Egyptians fought with determined bravery, replying to the hot fire poured into their forts from our heavy guns until they must have been quite decimated. . . ."

[4] For the above information see Parliamentary Papers, Egypt, No. 17.

to open fire on the works unless they were immediately stopped.
This was followed in a few hours by another ultimatum stating that
unless there was a temporary surrender of the forts for the purpose of
disarmament the British would open fire in twenty-four hours.
A hurried meeting took place at the Palace of Ras at Tin on the

CHAPTER IX

AS THEY SAW IT

THE following pages are given in my grandfather's own words:
Knowing that the firing was to begin at seven a.m., we took
care to be on the look-out; with a good telescope we could recognise
several of the larger men-of-war, the Helicon and the P. & O.
refugee steamer Tanjore. The morning was beautifully clear with
a light North-West breeze blowing. Exactly at seven a.m., we saw
a large puff of smoke rise in perfect silence and spread like a balloon.
In a few seconds came the heavy report of the gun which echoed
and re-echoed behind us.

Nothing further that we could see happened for a quarter of an
hour except that on the rising ground immediately at the back of
our works a considerable number of Bedouin made their appearance,
some armed with guns and swords, others with sticks; from their
position they could overlook a part of our premises. They had
increased to about 500 by nine o'clock, when fortunately a ricochet
shell fell among them, and although it did not burst, they all disappeared and kept at some distance. Just before that, one of them
fired a gun as we supposed, at some of our people, for the bullet
was heard whistling overhead, so we were glad to see them dislodged,
although the shell was suggestive of what might have happened had
it fallen 300 yards shorter, when it would have pitched into our engine
house.

At a quarter past seven, a tremendous volley, apparently from
the whole fleet, made the place shake. From that time until about
five p.m., with more or less intensity, but almost without inter-
mission, heavy firing continued; at times the smoke entirely hid
the ships and the town from us, but soon the wind increased and we
had a good view. We could see the flash from the ships' guns, and
the cloud of dust raised by the shell striking the fort or the ground,
showed about the time the report reached us.

About ten a.m., we were on the ridge of the engine house roof,
our highest point, when a shell passed over our heads, and after
hearing its screeching whirl, we felt the movement of the air from
it quite distinctly. I said that I thought it was time we got out of this,
and we scrambled down over the roof in much less time than it

took us to get up. Just before this a ricochet shell passed over our entrance gate, and I saw its splash in the water of Lake Mareotis about a mile beyond us, from this time until noon, shells were passing over us pretty freely, but few of them appeared to burst. I have since heard this much complained of by officers, both naval and military, but I never felt called on to join the non-contents on this subject, my own impression being that had all the fuses been unimpeachable, it might have been recorded of some of us, "That the subsequent proceedings interested them no more."

We had forgotten to make a proper provision of barley for my two horses; the groom told me he could get some. I let him go to Kom al Dik a little before seven a.m., and hoped he would return before the bombardment had made much progress. About eight a.m. I was standing near the entrance gate and saw him driving up making a great noise and followed by two Bedouin who were trying to stop him; fortunately I had a loaded gun in my hand, and when they saw me aiming at them, they fell back, otherwise I should certainly have seen my horse and trap taken off before my eyes, the groom and the Bedouin had already exchanged pistol shots just outside the Rosetta Gate; they were anxious to get horses to carry off the hoped-for plunder.

I had heard that there was a tacit understanding that in order to avoid unnecessary damage to the town, the ships would not fire on the Kom al Dik Fort unless it opened on them, but although we saw no shot fired from the fort during the day, one of the ships opened fire on it.

About the middle of the day, being tired and hungry, I went to my house to lunch, and was surprised and annoyed to find no preparation for anything to eat. On enquiry, I found the cook had prepared something for us, but he and the waiter were loafing about in a listless sort of way, apparently very much frightened; they evidently did not think of laying the table as usual, and seemed surprised when I told them that it would be better for them if this were done with as little delay as possible. About this time the firing was unusually heavy, and often the house shook with the concussion of the air; the waiter looked green and sometimes fairly had to lean against a piece of furniture for support, and it was only by the aid of a liberal volley of abuse that I was able to get either of the servants to do anything. A few hours later they could stand it no longer, and both of them climbed over the wall and disappeared, but they were considerate enough to leave a small supply of cooked provisions.

About 2 p.m. I could see the Inflexible, the Temeraire, and a three-masted ship, either the Alexandra or Superb, keeping up a tremendous fire on Fort Pharos; we could easily recognize the much heavier thunder of the Inflexible's 81-ton guns. I noticed one shot in particular from that ship; I saw the flash and then noticed that the shell touched on the parapet of the fort, thence it bounded across the Eastern harbour, considerably more than a mile, and struck on the shore near the Chatby Railway Station, I then lost trace of it for a few seconds until I heard a tremendous thud which shook the whole place, and saw a large cloud of dust rise about 200 yards to my right. We thought this quite near enough to be unpleasant, and were very glad to see that the next few shells were stopped at the fort itself. This fort had a mosque, with a minaret, which appeared to be melting away like a piece of ice in the sun.

During the afternoon we were surprised to see a carriage driving past the gate. It stopped at the door of our neighbour, a Frenchman, and one of the principal owners of hired carriages in Alexandria. I afterwards found that this carriage contained a police officer sent to take my neighbour to the town, where he was wanted by the Chief of Police; he, no doubt wisely, thought that discretion was the better part of valour, and instead of going out at the front gate to join the police officer, he escaped at the back, and climbed over the wall into my garden. He was dressed in what the French are pleased to consider a costume suited to the chase, and wore an enormous leather belt which carried a ten-barrelled revolver, a dagger on one side and a large cavalry sabre on the other, he also had a double-barrelled gun in his hand. All these arms were about as rusty as an old horse-shoe, and if the gun or pistol were to be used, it was a question quite open to argument, as to whether the greater danger would be in front or behind. Our neighbour greeted us with the assurance that he had come to give us a "coup-de-main" in case of need, he remained with us until matters had settled down a little, and often did good service by standing near an unprotected part of our outer fence.

I managed to get a good idea of the buildings which had been struck, and was surprised to find that so little damage had been done in the town. The worst news I heard, as to the truth of which there could be little doubt, was that soldiers had broken into many houses where there were Europeans, and on the pretence that they were signalling, they, in some cases, murdered the inmates, and in others, cruelly ill-treated them. I afterwards saw several of these poor people, and wondered that human beings who had been so knocked about could be still alive. One little Effendi who came to report to me, told me that he had hidden away his wife and family in the passages under our reservoir at Kom al Dik, and had passed the day with them. He seemed proud to have thought of so good a place, and said he had recommended it to all his friends.

About 6 p.m., we drove down as in the morning, to the Mahmoudia pumping station, and left a European there for the night, taking away the one who had passed the day there, and a very disagreeable day he had found it. The people we met about there seemed more hostile than in the morning, and though they had evidently been much frightened, we drove off amid a volley of curses against the "dogs of Christians" . More than once I had my finger on the trigger of a revolver pointing at a man hanging on to the carriage, but when they saw that the first to attack would have a bad time of it, they let us go on. It was a dark night with a cloudy sky, very unusual at this time of year, and no doubt caused by the heavy firing.

The close of the day appeared to be the signal for crowds of people to leave the town. Some seemed to be waylaying and robbing others in the open space outside our gates, and howling and shrieks continued through the night. About 10 p.m. one of our Arabs from the Mahmoudia station came to tell me that field guns and ammunition were being taken up the banks of the canal, a considerable quantity of the latter was stowed near our pumps, and an officer had told them to stop the engine. They tried to argue with him, but he replied "If the fire is not drawn in five minutes, one of you will have his throat cut and the other will be hung to the engine-room beam," pointing to a convenient place; this convinced them that further argument might lead to unpleasant results, and I have no doubt the fire was drawn without unnecessary loss of time.

I calculated that we had water enough in our intermediate canal to keep our main pumps going twelve hours, but as I was very uncertain when I might be able again to start the Mahmoudia pumps, I determined to keep this water for use by day instead of wasting it at night, so I stopped pumping from 10 p.m. until 5 a.m. on the 12th, when we started again. At daylight I sent an Arab messenger with a letter to Zulficar Pasha, whom I addressed as Governor of Alexandria, though I was very doubtful whether any such official now existed. I knew, however, that if he could be found he would do anything he could to keep the water supply going.

About 9 a.m. I was told that a Bey wanted to see me at the gate, I was rather suspicious, but went there, taking care to be well armed. I found it was Hassan Bey Sadek, the Sub-Prefect of Police, a man whom I had known several years, and in whom I had much confidence; he said, "The Khedive sends me to enquire how you are, and to thank you much for remaining at your post, we have heard that your Mahmoudia pumps are stopped. Can I do anything for you?"

I explained the matter to him, and he said, "I am much afraid I have no power, but if you will send an Arab with me I will do what I can." In about an hour he returned, and contrary to my expectation, told me the engine fire was being lighted, and he had been able to arrange the matter with the officer, who was fortunately an acquaintance of his. I was very pleased, and the arrangement held good to such an extent that our people were no more molested. I enquired for the Khedive and his suite, asking who were with him, he told me, and added, "Soldiers are all round the Ramleh Palace, and we do not know whether the Khedive is a prisoner or not; I am allowed to circulate, but I am much afraid it will all end badly. Why don't the English land? No one would now oppose them."

Through the night the town was in perfect darkness, not only no gas was lit, but there were no fires, only occasional rays of electric light from the top of some of the men-of-war throwing a fitful light around, which when it left, appeared to make everything darker than before.

The first Egyptian troops we noticed leaving the town in any numbers, marched out of the Rosetta Gate at 11.45 a.m. They marched quickly, and although the first 500 or so were in some sort of line, they did not appear to stand much on the order of their going; they took the Ramleh Road, and were followed by some 1500 more in gradually increasing disorder, until they became confused with the rabble who crowded the roads. Up to about 2 p.m. we did not notice any plunder being carried out of the town, either by soldiers or the crowd.

This exodus no doubt started immediately firing commenced

on the second day. Both soldiers and civilians had evidently had quite enough of being under fire, and I believe that if the firing had continued a few hours longer the town would have been empty, before the people had had time either to burn or plunder. But when they began to see that there was no more firing or risk of danger from delay, they bethought themselves of the good opportunity offered, and nearly all who came out after 2 p.m. were heavily laden with spoil.

From 2 to 5, we noticed several trains leaving the Moharem Bey Station, the carriages were crammed with people, both inside, on the steps, and on the roofs, even the buffers were crowded.

At about 4 p.m. some soldiers returned into the town, and the struggle to force their way toward the Rosetta Gate against the stream of the crowd pressing out of it was intense. Many people carrying bundles were upset, and a large number of soldiers finding it too difficult to get back, contented themselves with seizing the loads of others who were coming out. As dusk came on it would be difficult to imagine a more fiendish scene. The large open space between the cemeteries and our works was crowded, chiefly with soldiers who were undressing themselves and wrapping round their limbs all sorts of rich stuffs of silks and satins torn from divans and chairs. Some had brought gilt sofas as far as this, but finding them too cumbersome, broke them to pieces, and took only the coverings.

About 4 p.m. we noticed several fires in the town, and by 11 at night many of these had joined, making the largest conflagration I had ever seen the flames at times lighting up the whole landscape, so that we could recognise all the prominent buildings in the town by this lurid glare.

Soon after dark the stampede from the town ceased, and we were left in comparative quiet; between 4 and 5 p.m. some of our people saw a carriage driving out of the Rosetta Gate surrounded by a cavalry escort, and we concluded that it was probably Arabi Pasha. By the evening all the soldiers must have left the town, as we did not see any going out with the rabble on the following morning.

Immediately outside the garden fence were two large earthenware jars, which the doorkeeper, to propitiate the crowd, kept filled with water, and with further consideration supplied them with a couple of old jam tins from which to drink. A large open space was in front of us, thick with dust, and crowded with as motley a crew as it was ever my fortune to see. The main road from the town to the canal passed twenty yards in front of us; the heat was intense. The temporary handlers of the jam tins evidently thought themselves favoured mortals, but the privilege required much patient waiting for. These stern patriots would unbend a little in anticipation of a drink, and could look unruffled at a "dog of a Christian", and even speak to him.

Most of these people were cursing their lot and abusing Arabi in no measured terms. Two men who waited some time had been more abusive and also more communicative than the rest; one said, "I have been robbed of everything I had," and continued with a long tale of woe. He had a large bundle round his shoulders covered with a loose cloth, and as he stopped to dip up some water the covering fell off, and showed some hundred or so of European silk and satin cravats, evidently stolen directly from a shop. We tried to chaff him about it, but he only turned and cursed us; his friend had a large roll of cashmere shawls tied round his waist; all had something or other which evidently did not belong to them.

When we saw any number of soldiers coming on, we prudently retired behind some bananas close by which gave good shelter. But they saw that we were well armed and could have made it uncomfortable for the first few of them; they were only acting in small numbers, and did not care to run any risk for the possible benefit of their neighbours. Shortly after, several of the best known carriages and horses were led past in front of us. My neighbour, the French supplier of hired carriages, knew them all and told me the name of their late owners with a certain cynical glee. After a while I noticed, coming in the distance, a large closed carriage drawn by a good pair of white horses; a negro sat on the roof, and by a long rope he had captive a good looking saddle horse with no harness other than the rope round his neck. I said to my friend: "Whose are those, no doubt they are also stolen?" He looked for a moment, then jumped frantically from his chair and cried out "Oh, mon Dieu, ils sont a moi—they are mine—they are mine—stop thieves! Robbers!" etc. etc. The negro was his own servant and as he slowly passed by he put his thumb to his nose and elongating both hands made a geste at his former master, which I thought would have sent him mad. "Ah, gredin," he said, and seizing his gun I thought he was going to shoot at the fellow. I believe he would have, had I not prevented him. The crowd, pleased by this little comedy, set up a regular howl, my worthy neighbour made for the fence as though he would climb over it, but I again interfered, and I feel sure that if he had got outside he would have been killed.

We then saw most of his carriages and horses file before us, but he soon put on the air of a martyr to the cause, and looked on quite stoically, though during the rest of the time he remained with us he was always thinking of it, and every now and then would involuntarily mutter, "Les gredins".

Thursday 13th July and the morning of the following day, went by without any event worthy of notice. The time seemed very long to us, and we spent it in vain conjecture as to what was most likely to happen next. On the evening of the 13th, the fire seemed to be still further on the increase, both in the town and the Moharem Bey suburb. We could see the house of an Englishman less than half a mile off in such a blaze that there could not be much doubt as to its total destruction.

The doorkeeper of our town office came to tell me that thieves had broken into the office and stolen all his money. They then closely examined him as to what might be in our safes, but decided finally not to waste their time in trying to break them open. Being I suppose dissatisfied with the result of their visit, they collected some cotton from a divan, poured petroleum over it, put it in the fan light over one of the entrance doors, and set fire to it; it was still smouldering when I visited the place on the morning of the 15th. Had the floor of the upper storey been of wood I believe nothing would have saved the building, but it fortunately happened to be composed of masonry arches.

The whole of that day, Bedouin and other thieves were constantly passing in front of our works to and from the town in such numbers that it would have been very dangerous for any Europeans to have gone outside, but no serious attempt was made to molest us. During and since the bombardment, my policeman had kept very quiet, I think his moral being had received an immense shock. He seemed to be lost in wonder as to who were his friends, and who his enemies. On the morning of the 13th, he appeared suddenly to recollect that his wife and family were in the town, and he was not unnaturally anxious as to what might have befallen them; although he had been with me nearly a month, this was the first I had heard of his having a wife and family. However, by way of making up for lost time, he said he must go at once in search of them, and he started off with two or three of our Arab workmen, who partly from curiosity, not altogether free I expect from the hope of plunder, said they wanted to look for their friends.

About two hours later, they came back, carrying the poor policeman who had his foot so badly wounded, that although he was carefully tended, he was unable to walk again for more than a fortnight. It appears he first tried to pass in through the Rosetta Gate but found it impossible; he then went to the Moharem Bey Gate, and after a considerable time succeeded in getting under the archway; there he was knocked down by a cart which ran over his instep, crushing it very badly. Luckily his friends were with him and brought him back; he afterwards heard that his family had disappeared, and he did not see anything of them again for some months.

During the bombardment, Jean Ninet who was also in the thick of it, tells how one of the first English shells fell, without exploding, into the fort behind Ras al Tin. An Egyptian infantry lieutenant ran up to it. "My brothers," he shouted, "come here, boys. Come and see a specimen of *insanieh* (humanity), perfected by the English!" And they all roared with laughter, as only an Egyptian peasant can, while they returned to face the fire.

At about 10 in the morning of 11 July the carts started rumbling from the forts to the cemeteries, carrying the bodies of the slain. Each cart was followed by a crowd of wailing women, waving their arms as they went. It was on meeting these, that Jean Ninet nearly met his end. "Dog of a Christian," howled the women. "Accursed European. Having killed our brothers, you come here to watch their mutilated bodies pass by. That pleases you. Kill him. Kill him. The infidel, the dog." He would certainly have been killed had not a police sergeant armed with a revolver, recognised him and freed him from the crowd.[1]

On 13 July, Colonel Chaillé Long, who had taken refuge in one of the American ships, decided to make the attempt to enter Alexandria. At five in the morning he and a friend went over the ship's side having hailed a small Greek boat that was passing by. They were anxious as they rowed along, not so much by the thought of what they might meet in the burning town, as by the piratical look of the boatman. Nor were they reassured by seeing plunder

[1] See Ninet, op. cit., pp. 175 and 178.

of all sorts stowed away in the boat. Instead of making for the quay, this man to whom they had confided their lives, made straight for a two-masted schooner manned by more Greeks—the very prototype of operatic pirates. The Americans made it plain to their boatman that if he approached that schooner by so much as a further yard, he would be shot. He hesitated. Then, shouting to his confederates not to wait for him this time, he rowed to the quayside.

On arriving safely in the city, Colonel Long found a number of French subjects outside his Consulate asking for protection as their Consulate had been destroyed and their Consul was still taking refuge at sea. They wanted passes to enter their homes from which they had fled during the bombardment. (Passes were a measure adopted to prevent further looting.) So on 15 July Colonel Long tells how he placed a table on the "side walk" in front of the American Consulate, and there, during two days, from early morning until late at night, issued passes to applicants. Ali, the irrepressible attendant was very proud of his new-found dignity and importance.

"Mr. Consul, please let the Khedive in America know how much I have done for these poor people," said he.

Some Greeks also landed as soon as the bombing ceased. They sent a force of 120 armed sailors into the town, with the Consul, Vice-Consul and Secretary, Messrs. Rangabe, Scotidis and Metaxas, respectively. This cavalcade brought with them two pumps and paraphernalia for putting out the fires which now ravaged the place— the work of robbers and ruffiians, for the most part. Their forethought was justified because the Greek Consulate caught fire even as they approached it. They were able to save both it and most of the Greek church nearby. Mr. Scotidis has left some vivid accounts of this march.

"All the shops had been forced into and sacked, and the road was full of boxes and empty cases which the pillagers had abandoned as they went. Five or six houses in this road were full of holes from the canon balls of the English fleet. Two or three enormous balls and pieces of shell choked the streets. The barking of dogs and despairing cries of cats (les hurlements des chiens, les miaulements désesperés des chats), which had had nothing to eat for eight days, deafened us. . . . At each step we ran the danger of being engulfed under the ruins of the burning houses which were crashing into the road with a tremendous noise. Explosions sent debris of reddened iron into the air, which, falling on the passers-by, gave them but the opportunity of dying by being asphyxiated, burnt or crushed."[2]

As soon as the English had control of Alexandria they set up a system of summary justice to deal with the robbers and incendiaries. A table was placed in front of the Mixed Tribunals and three officers formed the court. Anyone caught looting or firing for the second time was taken a short distance off and hanged from a tree or shot. Hearing the accusation and the witnesses, getting the statements translated through an interpreter, condemning the prisoner to death and carrying out the sentence, was a matter of some twenty minutes per case.

When my grandmother, Mrs. Cornish, brought her five children back from Beirut, where they had taken refuge during the bombardment, there were still bodies hanging round the main square through which they had to drive to regain their home at the Waterworks. My mother just remembers sitting in the little open, basketwork carriage which fetched them from the harbour. Whenever they passed some unpleasant sight my grandmother would say: "Now, children, eyes right", or "eyes left", which ever fitted the case; most of them were young enough to think this was some new form of military game invented as a pastime.

In consequence of these scenes of ruin, the European communities were thinking ahead to the complicated question of compensation, as evidenced in *The Times* of 14 July: "One result is certain to come out of this awful disaster. A long series of claims will be made against Egypt for the loss of property. Even before their departure, in all the hurry of their exodus, each European owner of either house or furniture made a statement of what he owned and lodged it at his Consulate. Many even, who had not insured before, went so far as to insure their goods and chattels, not because they thought the companies would indemnify them from loss at the hands of a mob, but because they would have an additional proof of what they held to be the value of their property. Poor Egypt has a melancholy future before her in many ways."

In England, vehement opinion was being daily expressed against armed intervention in Egypt. Mr. John Bright, then Chancellor to the Duchy of Lancaster, felt it his duty to retire from the cabinet, so strong were his convictions that the bombardment was morally unjustified.

[2] *L'Egypte Contemporaire et Arabi Pasha* by N. Scotidis, Paris, 1888, pp. 196 and 197. A Greek edition also exists.

CHAPTER X

THE LOOTERS AND THE LOOTED*

ON 13 July, as Colonel Chaillé Long was letting himself overboard into the arms of the Greek pirate, and my grandfather Cornish was passing the time of day with the crowds by the Waterworks, Canon Davis, the Chaplain of St. Mark's Church, Alexandria (who was then in England), wrote a letter to his old friend, my grandmother Rowlatt:

"The awfulness and suddenness of this fearful blow in Alexandria makes me sad at heart. All is destroyed, of that there can be no doubt, and my long and happy career in Egypt is over. I fear, I fear that months *may*, certainly *must*, elapse before the country is reduced, and the war expenses will eat up all the revenues. I have not had a *single line* from anyone and the suspense is terrible.

"What does Mr. Rowlatt think of the position? Who could *ever* have anticipated such an awful issue as this? You ask about my iron box. It is, (or was) in the strong room of the Bank of Egypt and, of course, is either burnt or plundered. Also, I daresay, my books, linen, and *all my sermons too*, will have perished. It is a fearful judgment; God give us all strength to bear it.

"I know not what to say or think or do for the moment. If Mr. Rowlatt has returned he will be able to tell me the latest view of the situation in London. . . . I have no heart to say more."

While poor Canon Davis could only contemplate the scene, my grandfather Cornish was still part of it. Between three and four in the afternoon of the 14th, he was told that English soldiers were passing the gates. All the workmen were much excited. He told the groom to saddle his horse, but after waiting some time, no horse came. The groom was so frightened at the idea of having to go to the English soldiers, that he had climbed over the wall and run away, and was never seen again, although he was owed several weeks' wages. After some little delay Cornish rode out and found Captain Allen in charge of a party of 150 marines; they had landed early in the morning, and had marched around the outskirts of the town. The weather was hot, the roads dusty, and they

* All information and quotations in this chapter are from **Parliamentary Papers, Egypt, No. 18**, unless otherwise stated.

were tired and disappointed to find that their provisions which were to have come by a shorter road across the town, had not yet arrived. My grandfather soon sent fire-wood, a kettle, and four or five lbs. of tea, with which to revive them.

"On the morning of the 15th", wrote Cornish, "I went into the town and found it the most melancholy sight one could possibly imagine; although I had watched the progress of the fire I was much astonished to see the damage which had been done in so short a time. Many of the principal streets were quite impassable, and even to a person knowing the town well it was not an easy thing to find one's way down to the quay. There were but few buildings standing round the square, except in hideous ruins; the trees were nearly all scorched, blackened and shrivelled up. Every now and then a tottering pile of masonry came down with a crash.

"Almost the only thing about the centre of the town which remained unchanged, was the statue of Mohammed Ali; the stern old warrior still bestrode his horse, which is delicately poised on two legs, and with a cynical smile on his lips, the old gentleman seemed to look down on the surroundings with ineffable disgust."

(At the time of writing today, Mohammed Ali still surveys Alexandria from the back of the same prancing steed. But when I last left Egypt, in 1955, I could not see his features clearly enough to be sure of his feelings. He would have still seen certain wry humour in the events but would have viewed them with far less disgust, I fancy, than in 1882.)

My grandfather lost no time in making touch with the British Navy. His own view was that Arabi's army would not return to attack, but the naval intelligence officers thought otherwise and again urged him to evacuate to safety, but again he refused. In the middle of the night, however, Cornish thought he had been mistaken to refuse, for a succession of loud reports in quick succession shook the house.

He sent round orders for all the Europeans on the place to go to the engine loft, and in about ten minutes they were there, armed and waiting. It was a dark night, but at intervals an electric light from one of the ships flashed a ray all round, which lit up the desert at the back of the works; it looked quite bare, and there were no more reports or any sign of an enemy.

Soon after daylight they went down to the Rosetta Gate and there found that the night's explosions had been caused by charges of gun-cotton fired by Royal Marines in order to blow up a bridge which crossed the moat close by. "Had this little operation been done by daylight it would have saved us some unnecessary anxiety and alarm," was my grandfather's later comment.

About noon on the 16th Captain Maud, R. N. came to the Waterworks and told Cornish that he intended riding in the direction of Arabi's retreat until he could actually see where his army was stationed; they had so many contradictory reports and false alarms, that he was determined to find out the truth. My grandfather joined the party which consisted of a guard of five or six sailors and four Egyptian soldiers of the Khedive's body-guard; all were well mounted on very good horses belonging to the Khedive. They rode fast and sometimes over rough ground; all the sailors kept their seats remarkably well, though some of them appeared to do so by means more allied to gymnastics than to the usual received notions of horsemanship. Every now and then a sailor's horse would bolt and rush past at full gallop, in a way which somewhat marred the martial effect of the cavalcade—according to my grandfather's description.

On the straight road which leads from the Ramleh Palace to the Rosetta Gate they saw a long string of carts and carriages approaching them and at the same time heard loud reports on the left. They found that the shots were fired by a party of bluejackets who had fitted up a Gatling gun on a railway truck and were making a preliminary trial with it, and that the procession consisted of the Khedive's luggage and private effects on their way back to the Ras al Tin Palace. The Egyptian officer in charge of the convoy was a polite man, but complained bitterly that his party had been fired on, and some of them had had a narrow escape; he said that as the English, who were his friends, were permitted to shoot about in this promiscuous fashion, he would feel reluctantly obliged to retire from active service until a better understanding was arrived at.

Further on, sailors of the reconnoitering party rode on ahead and were surrounded by fifty or sixty Egyptians who appeared to be hustling them. The Captain gave the order to "make ready" with revolvers. The party rode in among the mob, and they scattered.

They next reached a canal bridge which had evidently been the scene of much fighting over stolen goods. Broken carriages and carts, bits of furniture and stuffs, dead animals, and many other things lay about in great confusion. Further on were human bodies in various stages of decomposition.

At a distance of thirteen or fourteen miles from Alexandria, Cornish noticed three white spots among the reeds to the left and said to the Captain, "Look out, those are soldiers." While he was taking out his field glass, about fifty men got up at a distance of three hundred to four hundred yards, unpiled arms and loaded. The Captain carefully surveyed the neighbourhood with his field glasses, but my grandfather reflected that as their group of a dozen horsemen stood on the railway bank about four feet above the general dead level, they must have offered a very conspicuous and tempting mark on the skyline.

The Captain then gave the order to retire, at which point one of his Egyptian Guards started at full gallop in the direction of Arabi's camp. "I think we had better give him a volley," said the Captain. But Cornish begged him not to do so thinking that it would bring on them the fire of the outposts, against which they could have done nothing with only revolvers. So he desisted, and that particular soldier of the Khedive joined Arabi's cause without mishap. The naval party swung round, started at a gallop, and did not slacken speed until they felt safe.

They were coming up to Alexandria at a hand-gallop in the dusk when they were challenged by the British outpost sentry. Captain Maud was a man of some six feet four and gifted with a voice in fair proportion to his size, but it took much parleying across the intervening space in the dark before the wary sentinel could be convinced that they were not enemies. Some friendly Egyptians were not so fortunate, being unable to explain themselves when challenged, several were fired on, and some wounded.

Next morning my grandfather visited the flagship with a curious but most welcome present for the Admiral—a block of ice found in one of the stores though the actual ice works had ceased to function. He then joined a party going on shore to cut the railway line outside the station, so as to prevent Arabi from taking away the rolling stock.

The most convenient place for cutting the line was under the bridge outside the station, where several Egyptian platelayers were sitting in the shade. Finding that Cornish spoke Arabic, and thinking from that that he was a man to be believed in, they at once set on with the work and with their help the marines soon lifted up two pairs of rails on each line. While this was being done an Effendi came out from the station, and begged them to wait five minutes until Arabi's engine, which was getting up steam, had gone out. Consequently the work was hurried on the more and in a few minutes it was impossible for an engine to pass. The Egyptian Administrator of the Railways was on the platform eating a water melon and expecting to start as soon as steam was up, probably intending to take the rest of the rolling stock with him. When he found out the situation, he mounted a carriage, drove to Ras al Tin, and arranged matters so comfortably with the Khedive's party that within a fortnight he was Governor of Alexandria.

On 18 July, Major-General Sir Archibald Alison landed and took over the command. He spoke to my grandfather about the difficulty of maintaining the water supply in the probable event of Arabi cutting off the Mahmoudia Canal. They spoke of the old Roman cisterns, and decided to examine them as soon as possible. A large gang was at work in a few days cleaning out and repairing several of them, till over 20,000 tons of filtered water were stored in about thirty of these cisterns. Still further precautions were taken to preserve the water of the Mahmoudia Canal. My grandfather was given a mounted guard under the command of Lieutenant Howard-Vyse, accompanied by whom he visited every steam engine irrigating the fields between the sea and Ramleh, and took away an essential piece of each in order to prevent their working. In some places the party were refused admittance, and had to break in, and at others the persons in charge tried to oppose them and only gave way when soldiers were marched into the buildings. They also went to all the water-wheels and warned the owners that any animals found working them would be shot without further notice. (Mr. Howard-Vyse was the first British officer to fall in the campaign, being killed in reconnaissance shortly afterwards.)

When the bombardment had ended Arabi and his men withdrew inland to the district of Kafr al Dawar where they encamped. As Arabi was leaving he saw Jean Ninet and called to him to join the doctors and the Red Crescent, and to follow. At Kafr al Dawar Arabi received a flow of visitors from far and wide, Sheikhs from Al Azhar in Cairo, local peasants, village headmen and distinguished leaders. Gifts also poured in, including a large tent which had belonged to Said Pasha, the late Khedive, and was presented to Arabi by Said Pasha's widow. This tent was captured at the battle of Tel al Kebir and taken by the Guards Brigade as a trophy of war.

Other noble ladies espoused Arabi's cause. One lady of the ruling house who supported him openly, spoke of him to Mr. Blunt and Lady Anne, five years later: "He was never a good enough soldier," she said, "and had too good a heart. Those were his faults. If he had been a violent man like my grandfather Mohammed Ali, he would have taken Tewfik and all of us to the citadel, and cut our heads off, and he would have been now happily reigning, or if he could have got the Khedive to go on honestly with him he would have made a great king of him. Arabi was the first Egyptian Minister who made the Europeans obey him. In his time, at least, the Moslems held up their heads, and the Greeks and Italians did not dare transgress the law. I have told Tewfik this more than once."[1]

Provisions in kind from farmers and merchants miles round, came in quantity to the Kafr al Dawar camp—grain, meat, vegetables, mules, camels and money. Many peasants had understood that Arabi was to usher in an era, the dawn of which would automatically cancel all debts due to European moneylenders. This undoubtedly roused the enthusiasm of some, but did not account for all the material and moral support given to Arabi by many of the poorer people.

Long years of ignorance and want among Egyptians partly accounted for further massacres of Europeans as they sought refuge in towns of the Delta inland from Alexandria. At Tanta horrible murders took place, but many were saved by the courage of a local Egyptian notable, Ahmed Minshawi Bey. He dashed into the scene with such determination, aided by a band of Bedouin, that he was able to rescue people by force. He followed this up by finding the hiding places of large groups of Europeans and seeing them safely escorted to Ismailia or Port Said. Nor was his the only case of such bravery. *The Times'* correspondent in Egypt received a petition from Franciscan Sisters and Monks, asking that British influence might be used to procure the release of a Bedouin Sheikh who had rescued them from massacre at Kafr al Zayat and treated them with courageous kindness but who had, none the less, been imprisoned.

On 22 July the Khedive Tewfik summoned Arabi to Alexandria.

[1] Reported in *Secret History*, op. cit., p. 394.

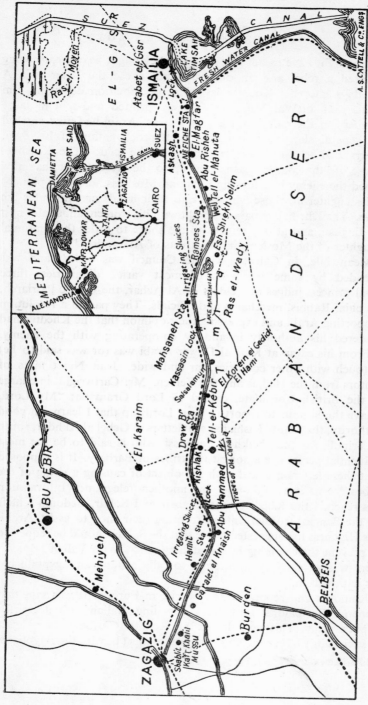

A map of the Tel al Kabir battle area as published contemporarily in the London press.

To go might have meant arrest, to disobey might have meant being declared a rebel and an outlaw. Arabi chose the latter risk. A few days later the Khedive issued a proclamation depriving him of his rank of War Minister. This was printed and sent in large numbers to the camp at Kafr al Dawar. Arabi had now entered the general slanging match and in a proclamation of his own, telegraphed to Governors of Provinces, he said: "The Khedive, whose life the country has spared up to the present time, has now joined the enemy in attacking Egyptian Moslems, and they plunder and slaughter all those who fall into their hands or who enter the town. The Khedive remains at night with his women, afloat amongst the English, and at day returns to the shore to order the continual slaughter of the Moslems in the streets of Alexandria."[2]

Meanwhile, in Cairo, a Grand Council was called, and was attended by some hundreds of most varied dignitaries—three royal princes, judges and elders of Al Azhar, the Coptic Patriarch, the chief Rabbis, merchants and officials. They passed a resolution supporting Arabi and expressing their opinion that the Khedive had rendered his authority invalid by co-operating with the enemy.

From his camp at Kafr al Dawar Arabi was (or was said to be) in touch with other countries, far and wide. Jean Ninet talks of visitors from the Hedjas and the Yemen. Mr. Cartwright, in charge of the British Consulate, cabled to Lord Granville: "My Lord, I have the honour to report to your Lordship that I learn, on good authority, that Arabi Pasha has sent letters to Gebel al Akhdar, south of Tripoli, for the Sheikh al Senoussi, who is said to be the most influential personage amongst the tribes of Barbary. It is supposed that these letters are sent with the object of causing a rising of the tribes." This was followed by another telegram: "Information has reached the Khedive that Zogheir and Sofair, Bedouin Chiefs on the Bengazi frontier, intend to bring their men to assist Arabi. His Highness has suggested to me that the Sultan should be requested to prevent their coming by dispatching orders to the Vali of Tripoli." Here was an early Arab attempt to rally around an Egyptian bid for nationalism.

Rumours and reports were also rife in Europe. It was said that General Garibaldi's sons were enrolling Italian volunteers for Arabi's army. This was denied by Renotti Garibaldi in a letter to friends in Florence: "Our sympathies must be with the Egyptians,

[2] Parliamentary Papers, Egypt, No. 17.

who are fighting for their independence," he said, "but no recruiting is going on, because we can do nothing for them at the moment, the difficulties we should have to encounter being too great."[3]

In England, the repercussions of the refugee problem were still much in evidence. The Lord Mayor continued nobly to collect such items as "A Lady's Thanksgiving for Peace and Safety in England" £10; Messrs. T. & J. Hollingsworth, £20; Lady Augusta Onslow, £20.

Lady Houlton, wife of The Chief Secretary to the Government in Malta, wrote to the papers saying: "The distress still continues and there is every prospect of its continuance (as practically shown on the occasion of my weekly distributions, when crowds of half-clad and destitute women and children wait at the store from sunrise to sunset), till such time arrives when Her Majesty's Government can with safety permit the return of the refugees to what has been for so many years their home."

[3] See *The Times*, 16 August 1882.

CHAPTER XI

MULES AND MEN-OF-WAR

THROUGHOUT the summer of 1882 the European Powers in general, and England in particular, wrestled with the Government of the Sultan of Turkey; and they wrestled too, with each other. Should Turkey be asked to help, or would they get on better without her? If she stepped in, how should she step in, and where, and why, and when? It was finally decided that England should follow up the bombardment by a military campaign to crush Arabi and that the Turks would land troops to give material assistance to the British Army, under the command of Sir Garnet Wolseley. Deciding on these points was one thing, but getting the Porte to comply was another. It had finally been arranged that the Turkish horse should be brought to the water; it had actually been brought there; it had intimated its readiness to drink; but still it did not, in fact, do so.

Some of the telegrams interchanged between Lord Granville and Lord Dufferin, H.B.M.'s Ambassador at Constantinople, show that it was not so much a matter of a horse, as of mules:

"The Consul at Smyrna reports that the mules which have been purchased in Asia Minor for the use of Her Majesty's Forces in Egypt cannot leave, because no permit has yet been received from Constantinople. Urge the Porte to send a Firman at once. The steamer is waiting, but cannot be detained after Saturday."

The British Government wisely had another string to their bow. Through the good offices of the English Consul at Naples a contract was concluded for the furnishing of 1,000 mules to be sent to Egypt and negotiations were started for the purchase of 1,800 draught oxen. The beasts were to be attended by Neapolitan muleteers and drovers, to be paid at the rate of 5 francs a day. But if the Sultan had promised mules, those mules had to come. So the telegraph wires hummed from London to Constantinople: "The delay in sending the order for the embarkation of the mules is most unfriendly. Use such language as you think best adapted to insist on Firman being sent at once." The Parliamentary Papers do not record Lord Dufferin's language, but we know that it failed of its aim.

116

The plot thickened. H.B.M.'s Ambassador found that the Porte had ordered the Governors of all provinces to prevent the export of mules or other animals which England might need in Egypt. Encouragement was telegraphed back to the Ambassador: "Her Majesty's Government entirely approve your action respecting the mules. If permission to export them is delayed, speak strongly as to the effect on relations between the two Governments." By 23 August a ray of hope broke in and Lord Dufferin was able to telegraph that the Turkish Foreign Minister had sent him word that the necessary permission would be given for the export of the mules, but he had added that this must be considered as unofficial. The next day brought still better news. Not only had the question of the mules been satisfactorily settled, but the release was reported of all the drovers, shepherds and others who had been put into prison by the Turkish authorities for having engaged themselves with persons who had contracted to supply the British Army with live meat.

When Lord Granville arrived at the Foreign Office on the following day, his hopes were to be dashed, for he read this: "I regret to have to inform Your Lordship that, although the Prime Minister and the Foreign Minister had actually written a letter ordering the release of the shepherds and muleteers engaged by the contractors to proceed to Egypt in charge of the live stock which had been shipped at Odessa and Smyrna for the use of our army, a subsequent order from the Palace has threatened with imprisonment the artificers who have undertaken to supply the contractors with the 600 pack-saddles we require."

On 7 September, Lord Dufferin was able to telegraph to Lord Granville: "The Ottoman Government is now showing a friendly spirit in regard to the exportation of mules, men and horses." Lord Dufferin had won through, though it must have added years to his life. But his respite only lasted a few days for on September 12th he had to send the melancholy news that a number of porters engaged for the army in Egypt had been imprisoned by the Porte and a servant of the British Consul-General who had nothing to do with the business, was among the persons arrested. No sooner was this conveyed by telegram to Whitehall when the news broke that the Consul's servant had been released on bail but that the person who stood bail for him had been put into prison.

Whoever this co-operative individual may have been, there

he seems to have stayed, for Lord Dufferin was by now in full negotiation about the number of Turkish troops to be sent and the exact point on the Egyptian coast at which they would embark. The correspondence on these matters reveal that they took place with all the same attendant difficulties as bedevilled the mules, the pack-saddles, the drovers and the Consul's servant. This detailed obstruction revealed a fundamental unwillingness to enter the lists with Europe against Arabi and his Moslem following.

Lord Dufferin was now instructed to see to another major issue. It was considered essential that the Sultan should declare Arabi a rebel before the British army could launch a head-on attack at him. After weeks of talk, a proclamation to this effect was eventually agreed upon. But instead of publishing it, the Turkish Foreign Minister approached Lord Dufferin a few days later to say that, after all it would be better if a proclamation of a different character preceded the one already agreed upon. "This repudiation of his former engagement made me so angry that I got up and left the room," reported Lord Dufferin.

The whole question had to be gone into afresh and in detail once again. Agreement however was reached and the draft duly submitted to Lord Granville. After careful scrutiny he inserted some words and expunged others and returned it, fully satisfied. The Turkish officials also expressed themselves as satisfied and a proclamation was indeed published in Turkish, with no further delay. But Lord Dufferin's sense of relief was again short lived; a word for word translation showed that the document published was quite other than had been finally accepted by both parties. Once more Lord Dufferin had to report to the Foreign Office on "this intolerable mode of procedure". Full scale negotiations about the exact wording broke out yet again. The phrase to which Her Majesty's Government really took offence was "finally to solve the Egyptian question so as not to give occasion for foreign intervention". On 7 September an English version of the revised Proclamation was published in *The Times*; a copy in Arabic was circulated throughout Egypt, and one version was sent by the English to India, where a considerable feeling had arisen in favour of Arabi.

Events had so dragged on at Constantinople that the British Army under General Sir Garnet Wolseley had by now been several weeks on Egyptian soil. Yet by the second week in September Lord

Dufferin was still hard at it in Constantinople negotiating the details, circumstances and conditions of the Turkish Expeditionary Forces to Egypt; in spite of the fact that the battle of Tel al Kebir had been already fought and won, Arabi defeated and imprisoned.

On 15 September Lord Dufferin received a summons from the Sultan to wait upon him at 3 p.m. On arrival at Yildiz he was shown into a room where there eventually assembled the Grand Vizier, the Minister of Foreign Affairs, the destined Commissioner for Egypt, secretaries, chamberlains and interpreters without number. The Sultan was seated in an adjoining apartment and the next eleven hours (from 3 p.m. to 2 a.m.) were spent in the delivery of various messages and proposals from the Sultan to Lord Dufferin and vice versa.

At one point Lord Dufferin ventured to observe that the march of events had completely changed the situation in Egypt, and that there was no longer any necessity for military co-operation whatso-ever.

Diplomatic activity on this vexed level did not take place only between Constantinople and London. Most of the major Chancel-leries of Europe were buzzing with it throughout the summer, for England was anxious that military intervention in Egypt should be on an allied basis. France was sounded on the point but replied that "the Ministers of War and Marine considered that the present season would be in all respects most unfavourable, and that, if military operations were undertaken before November, at least half of the troops employed would perish from sickness". France was, in short, averse to it.

Even before the bombardment of Alexandria, the Suez Canal began to feature in official pages as a possible complication. The problem started pianissimo, on 10 July but slowly mounted in pace till, some weeks later, the Grand Concert of Europe was giving free play to its full crescendo—the castinets of Spain, the fiddles of Italy, the shrill wind instruments of France, the pipes of Portugal, and the big drums of Great Britain. Turkey, perhaps exhausted by her midnight sessions in the Yildiz Kiosk with Lord Dufferin, does not seem to have been in the orchestra; but some-where, muffled in the middle of the noise, those who were not too occupied with manipulating their own instruments, could have faint-ly heard the voice of Egypt herself, had they listened.

Monsieur de Lesseps was in Paris and was agitated. He was too agitated to put a date on his letter to the British Ambassador to France. "My dear Ambassador," he writes, "in view of events in Egypt I think I should communicate to you the following instructions which I have telegraphed to the superior agent of the Suez Canal Company at Ismailia: All action or warlike demonstration is forbidden at the entrances or approaches of the Maritime Canal. Its neutrality was proclaimed by the Firman of Concession. It has been acknowledged and practised during the two last wars, the Franco-German and the Russo-Turkish. It would be useful if each maritime Power interested in the free transit of the Suez Canal could send a man-of-war in an observing capacity, to Port Said."

The British officials in Egypt wrote to Lord Granville on the same day saying that the Royal Naval Commanding Officer at Port Said had demanded permission to patrol the Canal with a torpedo boat, but that the Canal Company had "not felt at liberty to grant the permission in view of the serious consequences which it might entail, bearing in mind that the Company is a commercial undertaking, is by law Egyptian, and therefore should not, by any action on the part of its officials, become involved in any political or military operations".

By 19 July, Monsieur de Lesseps was in Egypt. "His presence in Egypt just now is rather unfortunate," commented the acting British Consul to the Foreign Office. Ten days later the Secretary of the Admiralty ordered Admiral Seymour to obtain permission from the Khedive Tewfik for the Royal Navy to act on his behalf in the Canal, and, if necessary, to hold for him all places on the Canal and the railway between Ismailia and Suez. Full powers were given by the Khedive. This news was a blow to de Lesseps, who telegraphed to his son Charles in Paris saying that if the English disembarked at Ismailia, where there was not a single Egyptian soldier, it would but be that they intended taking possession of the Canal. "The invaders will find us," he cabled, "without arms, at the head of our personnel, in front of them to bar their way with protests."

Charles de Lesseps took this telegram to the British Suez Canal Directors at their headquarters in Paris where he urged them not to infringe the neutrality of the Canal and said that, if they did so, it would create a precedent for the future which Great Britain might have to deplore. He pointed out the fact that Arabi Pasha had hitherto respected the neutrality of the Canal, and maintained that he would continue to do so as long as the Canal was not made use of by any hostile Power for the furtherance of its designs.

The Directors, in their turn, pointed out that they did not share de Lesseps' confidence in Arabi's intentions. They looked upon the need to occupy the Canal as an action forced on Her Majesty's Government, not because of any aggressive designs, but on behalf of the legitimate Government and ruler of Egypt. Nothing they said, however, had any effect on Monsieur Charles de Lesseps who maintained, to the end, that the neutral character of the Canal was of greater importance to England than to any other country and that her proposed action in that zone would be calamitous.

Arabi was also in touch with de Lesseps on the subject of the Canal, assuring him that its neutrality would not be violated by the Egyptians except as a last expedient if the English committed some act of hostility at any point from Port Said to Suez. According to Jean Ninet, the Egyptians had everything prepared to cut the Suez Canal in four places, and most of Arabi's council were eager to do this; but by Arabi's express orders the dynamite was withdrawn and the plan abandoned.

On 20 August Lloyds agent at Port Said telegraphed that British troops had landed there and that entry into the Canal was forbidden by the English at both ends.

European reactions to this were varied. The *République Francaise* observed: "The British Cabinet will not fail to find excuses, and, to be just, we must admit that it can invoke some very specious ones. In the first place the road to India was threatened; at least, it can pretend so. . . . The English have raised relatively considerable military forces, have gone to enormous expenses, and staked the honour of their flag and arms. Whose fault is it if they are reduced to choosing between compromising the success of their great effort by adhering to the letter of treaties or profiting by the opportunity to seize a substantial guarantee?. . .Are treaties respected nowadays?" The *République Francaise* then gives three instances in which it considers that France, England and Austria broke agreements between the years 1856 and 1877. The comment of *The Times* Paris Correspondent on the situation was: "England has gone to work, and she has no more violated treaties in occupying the Suez Canal than a fireman violates individual privacy by breaking into a house on fire." Not a forest fire in 1882—just a house. Berlin praised the occupation of the Suez Canal as a most skilful strategical combination. It acknowledged that the English Commander-in-Chief had played his cards exceedingly well in deceiving the enemy and had succeeded almost without loss, in taking possession of the Suez Canal, "which was the principal aim of the whole campaign, and to secure there the most valuable basis for his further operations". The German press stated that no Power, not even Russia, had protested against the occupation of the Suez Canal, but they all acknowledged that England had, in this case, acted under *force majeure*, and that she was entitled to do so, as she had expressly reserved to herself the right to use the Suez Canal for her military operations.

Letters to the Press from private individuals and societies were manifold during the summer. The alternative route round the Cape was commented upon for and against, our action was upbraided, justified, or taken for granted. "It is difficult to account," says a letter in *The Times* of 12 August, "for the nervous excitement now witnessed, which, it seems, *Eau de Suez* has intensified instead of calmed." The French Society for the Friends of Peace let themselves go in a single majestic sentence addressed to Monsieur de Lesseps: "If the spirit of our Association, and the principles it has assumed the task of propagating, make it our duty to blame the arbitrary and violent act by which agents of military force, for a time at least, have laid hands on an essentially pacific and international work, invested by public law with the character of neutrality a work which ought to be for all civilized nations, especially for trading nations, an object of inviolable respect, we also have the satisfaction in warmly congratulating you on the noble firmness and courageous dignity with which, first you, and after your example a personnel imbued with your spirit, have in this critical situation defended the cause of law, civilization, property, peace, etc., and we may add, without exaggeration or flattery, the cause of the creative spirit against destructive force."[1]

Spain soon entered the lists, though in rather a hesitant fashion, for Madrid opinion varied as to how efficient a force could be raised by Spain to co-operate with vessels of other Powers. Yet she eventually sent out a selection of men-of-war to watch over Spanish interests in Egyptian waters—the Concordia, the Maria de Medina, the Carmen and the Zaragossa all set forth. Whereupon Mr.

[1] *The Times*, 9 September.

Walter Baring, representing England in Lisbon, sent a despatch to Lord Granville, the subject of which might have been guessed by his Lordship even before it was read: "My Lord, in an interview which I had today with the Minister of Foreign Affairs, the conversation turned upon the Suez Canal. His Excellency said that. . . Portugal had no wish to push herself forward in any way, but when the Government heard that measures had been proposed for securing hereafter the safety of the Canal, in which France and Holland were to take part, they thought that the voice of Portugal should also be heard. . . ."

Meanwhile, the summer's events in the town of Suez itself had led to an almost total evacuation of the British residents, who took refuge afloat. The British Consul then reported that whenever he went on shore he found the town perfectly quiet and that the Governor of Suez, Hussein Pasha Sirri, showed the greatest desire to keep order. On 29 July H.M.S. Euryalus arrived at Suez and Admiral Sir William Hewett deputed the Consul to find out from the Egyptian Governor whether he was a follower of the Khedive or of Arabi. This was a question on which the Governor was plainly unwilling to give a decided answer, at least he was unwilling to give it to the Englishman. When further pressed by the Consul, he told the Admiral that he was loyal to the Khedive. This was at 10 p.m. At midnight a railway engine with one carriage arrived and was immediately surrounded by soldiers who kept off all comers. Soon afterwards the Governor entered the carriage and this one carriage train started immediately for an unknown destination. The result was that there was a stampede of local Egyptians from Suez under the impression that the Governor had left because the English were coming and that they would all be murdered.

The one or two remaining Egyptians in Suez, if literate, could have read the following proclamation from the British Admiral translated into Arabic and stuck up on a wall.

To the inhabitants of Suez, being Egyptian subjects:

It is hereby made known to you that the town of Suez has this day been occupied by British forces in the interests of His Highness the Khedive, your lawful Ruler.

You have no reason for fear if you conduct yourself in an orderly manner, but if there is any molestation of British subjects,

or of any other foreign European subjects, I shall take the necessary repressive measures.

You must let all Egyptians know that the rumours spread by
the rebel Arabi Pasha, who has been removed by His Highness
the Khedive from the post of Minister of War, that the intention
of the British in occupying Egypt was to murder the Mussulman
population, is utterly false, and without any foundation whatever.
We came here to restore order and peace to your country, and
wish to be your friends.

Bring us anything you have to sell and we will buy of you,
and you will soon thank me for coming to Suez.

The note struck at Ismailia, in connection with these events,
was keyed to a higher pitch than that of Suez. The *Standard* of
25 August printed an item cabled from its Ismailia correspondent,
which reported that Monsieur de Lesseps, his son, and a party
had just returned from a ball at 3 o'clock in the morning. All
had been quiet, there was not an Egyptian soldier in the town, and
perfect confidence was felt that the war could not approach this
portion of Egypt. On a sudden the stillness of the night had been
broken by a rush of armed men firing wildly in all directions. A
gardener of de Lesseps and two employees of the Company had been,
without the slightest offence on their part, shot dead. "Such was
Monsieur Victor de Lesseps' version of the events which attended
our occupation of Ismailia," commented the correspondent.

This news item did not go unnoticed by the Lord Commissioners
of the Admiralty, who told the Foreign Office on September 1st
that although their Lordships did not usually take notice of the
reports which were circulated through the press, and that they did
not attach very much importance to the repetition of a conversation,
yet they thought it desirable to repeat the telegram to Admiral Sir
Beauchamp Seymour, and request him to report back his own
account of the occupation of that place.

It is plain from the official naval reply that the British forces
thought Ismailia was garrisoned by Arabi's troops, and for that
reason they had opened fire.

Monsieur Victor de Lesseps was the Canal Company's agent in
Egypt at that time and in his own report to the Canal Company's
President in Paris he tells of his interviews with the British Admirals. .

"I had no difficulty in convincing Admiral Hewett that he had overstepped the limit of rights due to a belligerent, as the act of force which he had committed against us had not even imminent danger as an excuse, but only an eventuality which might not happen, that of the cutting of the Sweet Water Canal which, up to now, had been respected by the Egyptians, in spite of the English landing, and out of consideration for the Company. I added that if the Egyptians heard that the English were occupying the Waterworks with the purpose of taking a considerable provision of water, to the detriment of the Company, it might be feared that the water would be cut, from one moment to the other.

"After which the Admiral asked me for explanations about the neutrality of the Canal, and on the reciprocal rights and duties of the Company and the Egyptian Government. I made him understand how much the attitude of Monsieur Ferdinand de Lesseps and of the Company was distorted [dénaturée] in England, how in defending the principle of neutrality which is the basis of the Concession, the Company showed itself as a friend of English interests, as it was trying to stop her committing acts which would be deplorable to general world commerce, and in consequence, to England's commerce, who is the Canal's principal client; that in protesting against the numberless violations of our Regulations committed by the Royal Navy, the Company were not showing hostility to the English nation, but hostility to certain acts, against which she would have protested with equal energy, if any other navy had been culpable of them."

If Victor de Lesseps found Admiral Hewett reasonable, his luck had turned when faced with Admiral Hoskins.

"The Admiral, wishing to hear nothing, interrupted me brusquely at every instant, and did not get beyond the two sentences: 'Monsieur de Lesseps is the enemy of England. I see the Egyptian flag here.' All my efforts to demonstrate to him that we were not the enemies of England and that the fact of the Egyptian flag flying at Port Said did not give the British Navy, any more than other Navies, the right to put themselves beyond the Regulations—all my efforts, I say again, were in vain. It was evident that the Admiral had decided that we were the enemies of England, and that Port Said and Lake Timsa were Egyptian waters where he was at liberty to act as he thought fit."

De Lesseps gives a lively description in his report of the next events.

"...During the night of the 19th-20th all the European population, the personnel of the Company and the principal Egyptian functionaries had gone to the home of Monsieur Poilpré, Head of the Domains Service, for a ball of the gayest, animated by the presence of officers from the Spanish and Austrian men-of-war. At two in the morning everyone returned home and began to sleep when, towards 3 o'clock in the middle of a very dark night, the streets rang with war cries, mingled with the rattle of fusilade and the rolling of cannon as they were dragged along. It was the English sailors landing, without having warned the inhabitants that they were liable to be killed in the streets. On what were they firing? On whom? No enemy faced them. The Egyptian camp was at Nefisha, 3 kilometres away from Ismailia. There were only a few police [soldats de police] in the town, most peaceful folk who had lived long in Ismailia, and who never had a thought beyond keeping order.

"Soon after the landing, the cannon thundered. It was Orion and Carysfort sending shells into Nefisha and the desert. The shooting continued in the streets of Ismailia.

"At daybreak, it ceased in the European town, with fortunately but one victim. He was a European, a Dutchman, M. Broens, who, not clearly answering the 'Who goes there?' of a sailor, received a shot at close range which went through his body and shattered his left arm. M. Broens is between life and death; the doctors consider his case is hopeless....

"On disembarking, the English cut our telegraph wires to Suez and Port Said. Captain Fitzroy occupied the offices of the port and our boats were seized. Ismailia is blocked and we do not know what is happening on the rest of the line.

"In the afternoon, we planned to take the families of our personnel to safety. As only 300 sailors occupied the town, and during the night, the Egyptians at Nefisha might have taken the offensive, it was but prudent to get the women and children afloat on the Lake. As to the personnel and Monsieur Ferdinand de Lesseps, they decided not to move from the town. Their families came to the appointed place. Captain Fitzroy opposed their departure.

"So I wrote him a letter. Mr. Fitzroy answered me verbally at 7 in the evening, when darkness was beginning, that the families were free but that Monsieur de Lesseps and all his personnel would spend the night in the town, for it was to be attacked, there would be a battle in Ismailia, and he wanted Monsieur de Lesseps and all the personnel to be there. 'I am master now,' said he. These odious words were rather gratuitous, seeing that Monsieur de Lesseps and all the personnel, heads and employees, had declared that they would not leave the town and that it was but a matter of the families. Some of the families preferred to go back to the town; the other party could then embark in boats sent by Don Carlo Ruiz, Commandant of the Spanish frigate Carmen, and by N. Blonfield, Commander of the Austrian cruiser, Albatross. Our refugees were hospitably received aboard these ships. . . ."

Mercifully M. de Lesseps had nothing but praise for his relations with the officers in command of the Army, who asked to be told of all claims which might ensue from the passage or stay of troops, which would be made good immediately. But one regretable incident took place with the Royal Marines. At kilometre 54 the commander of the detachment took over the water supply and wished to expulse the daughters of the head of the station, as he considered that they used too much water. The most severe orders were given by the English Authorities that such a thing should not happen again.

Monsieur de Lesseps avowed that during the days of the 20th and 21st the movement of the English ships, without pilots, gave rise to complete confusion: "Most of them were stuck and several had to disembark their troops on the bank above Ismailia, being incapable of drawing out on their own resources. Admiral Seymour had to acknowledge it and the pressure he put upon us, on the 21st, to give our services, is proof of it.

"It is fitting to add that the British naval authorities tried to obtain the services of several of our pilots, not through their chiefs, and that all the pilots, without exception, refused to move without the Company's orders; they even resisted some attempts at enticement."

At least some of the above misunderstandings might have been avoided if the communication warning the Canal authorities of England's forthcoming action, had been received before, and not after, active operations for the occupation of the Canal had actually begun.

Among the many tensions of those taut summer days was a brisk exchange of opinion between the Government of India in Simla and the Secretary of State for India in London. The latter had proposed that Indian Revenues should bear all expenses of the Indian contingent preparing for military operations in Egypt.

This instantly produced the strongest possible protest from Lord Ripon, the future Lord Cromer and others on behalf of India. They sent a many-paged despatch expressing their pained surprise to Lord Hartington, the Secretary of State for India in London. It pointed out that the Indian Government had not been consulted on the guiding principles of policy towards Egypt, and were, even then, in total ignorance of any plans save what they read in the public press.

The interests of India, they affirmed, did not call for armed intervention. "We are entrusted with the administration of India," the despatch continued, "we are in close contact with the Indian people, we are in a position to watch the currents of public opinion in India, we are directly responsible for the tranquillity of the country and it seems to us therefore that we are better able than any one in England, however eminent or experienced, can possibly be to judge of the financial and political effects and bearing of a message so important to Indian interests as of a sudden and unexpected demand for a long and indeffnite war contribution.

"We can scarcely conceive any subject upon which the Government of India, as representing however imperfectly the people of this country, can have a clearer or better claim to be heard."

The authors of this despatch then outlined the difficulties and injustices that would arise "if any direct tax were imposed with the express object of meeting the charges of a war which in the opinion of the tax payers, that is to say in this case the most influential classes of India, should not be borne by the people of India at all, but by the people of England". Those long Victorian sentences may seem onerous to modern ears, but the recipient could be left in no doubt as to their meaning. They carried conviction for they were written by men who spoke their mind without fear or favour.

The English Government had greatly to temper their original proposal. In due course they paid a substantial sum themselves towards covering the cost of Indian participation in the Egyptian campaign.

CHAPTER XII

CLIO, THALIA AND MELPOMENE*

WHILE these extensive and varied projects were being unrolled in Suez, Paris, London and Constantinople, old Jean Ninet, the Swiss, aged 65, was in camp with Arabi. He describes Arabi's reactions to the possibility of being branded a rebel. Arabi thought that the Sultan of Turkey would never call him a rebel, "except by force or treachery, if England or France put the foot on the throat", he said. "And even if it happened, of what worth would that concession be, dragged forth by fear, and contrary to the logic of facts? Nothing! But the newspapers of Europe," continued Arabi, "are they then as sheep who run behind the ram with the bell round its neck? Because *The Times*, the *Débats*, and the *République Francaise* call me a rebel, have all the other papers to repeat, like a lot of parrots, 'Arabi, the rebel'?" And then turning and smiling at the officers who sat in a circle round him: "You know the fate which awaits rebels. They are shot, there where they are found, on the field of battle. When all is said and done, as long as we are here, according to 'Samour', rebels is our name; if history passes us by, the shot will not miss us."[1] (*Samour* was the nearest Arabi could get to the name, Seymour. The word *samour* in Arabic means a marten.)

On 16 August General Sir Garnet Wolseley landed his expeditionary force in Egypt. The Egyptian soldiers were wont to penetrate the English camps at night to see what they could lift. They brought back spiked white helmets, empty drinking flasks, and once, some pairs of uniform trousers. The Egyptians were much entertained at the ideas of soldiers removing their uniform to sleep, though the damp summer heat would make such a course more than understandable. In addition to these occasional forays the Egyptian army set about throwing up extensive earthworks.

One August morning great excitement ran through the camp. It was said that a group of captured English sailors were about to

* Unless mentioned otherwise, all information and quotations in this chapter come from Parliamentary Papers, Egypt, No. 18; Indian Contingent (Egypt) (Expenses) 1883; East India (Transport of Troops to Egypt), 1884.

[1] *Arabi Pasha*, op. cit., p. 227.

arrive. Sure enough, a cavalcade of camels loomed in the distance accompanied by a curious crowd of Egyptian hangers-on. Eight sailors and four officers not unlike Englishmen formed the centre of the party. Arabi and his men gathered in the great tent and seated the officers in front of them. Jean Ninet was asked to translate, but the prisoners spoke no English. Ninet, trying German, Italian and French soon found them to be Austrians who had been on their way from Port Said to Alexandria to join the Austrian Imperial Yacht which had arrived there. It took much explaining before Arabi was convinced of the misunderstanding; but the prisoners were fed and released.

On another occasion an outlying guard brought in a young European man, totally naked. On arrival at the camp the Egyptians outfitted him temporarily in a table cloth having made a hole in the centre for his head. He was so miserable and in pain, that no one had the face to laugh at this spectacle. He turned out to be an Italian deserter, one Paolucci by name, from the frigate Castalfidardo anchored in the port of Alexandria. The young man was kindly treated. He said he had deserted to join the cause of the Nationalists. Be that as it may, he was certainly in need of care for he had been hiding for five days in the salt marshes, among the reeds inland from the sea, and his limbs were so swollen that every movement hurt. He was given clothes and sent to Cairo where he stayed till the English arrived there, who then handed him over to the Italian authorities.

Amid these anecdotes of prisoners and supposed prisoners, a Reuter's telegram from Alexandria was published in *The Times* on 29 July. It reads thus: "A loyal native who has arrived from Cairo, via Port Said, states that a number of natives dressed in European clothes, with white helmets, have been paraded through the streets as English prisoners and taken to the Kasr al Nil barracks." Probably no one but the "loyal native" himself, knew what degree of truth there was in this report.

One day, however, a real English midshipman, called de Chair, was captured while on a foraging sally in Ramleh. Jean Ninet describes him as being fair, beardless and a child, dressed in an untidy uniform and heavy boots, and carrying a small sword. His face was intelligent and gentle; he behaved with dignity but looked far from reassured when Arabi asked him to take a seat within a few paces of himself, among a great crowd of Egyptian officers and Bedouin. But he was more at his ease when Arabi questioned him kindly and with deference.

Towards the end of the audience, Arabi (who during the action of the fleet had thought he read the word "Alexandria" on one of the bombs) said to young de Chair: "It would be difficult to deny the premeditation of the bombardment of Alexandria; all that happened, proved it. Even your shells, which had on them the name of the town destroyed, show it." To which the young man replied, "It wasn't properly read. The inscription was not Alexandria but Alexandra, the name of the ship which fired it, and which is also the name of Princess Alexandra."

Apparently everyone looked astonished but convinced. Arabi thanked the prisoner saying: "Ah well! I understand. My error is excusable, for I do not know English. But it seems a strange idea to call a metallic and murderous monster by the name of a young and beautiful lady. Tell Mr. de Chair that he must have seen that we are not the brigands and bands of assassins of which they must certainly have told him in England and in Egypt. What he sees around him, are the people, it is the Egyptian nation in arms, lifted against atrocious Turkish-Circassian oppression which is upheld today, by the great and liberal England." "I own," said the young man, "that what I read in the newspapers and have heard from my chiefs, is very different from what I have before my eyes. But I am a Service-man and my duty is to obey, without saying anything."[2]

Arabi then asked about the boy's parents: "They will be afraid to hear you are with man-eating Arabi." He next enquired if de Chair preferred staying there or returning to his ship. The boy replied that he preferred the ship, as he had work to do. "Excellent," said Arabi, "you prefer work to idleness. Meanwhile you shall go to Cairo," and he gave careful orders for his good treatment.

The arrival of Midshipman de Chair in Cairo, at 2 o'clock in the morning, caused a great sensation. People came with torches and lanterns and accompanied the closed carriage in which the prisoner was placed, shouting that the Sultan had gained a victory over the English, they being under the impression that the prisoner was Admiral Seymour. Facilities were given for his mother to correspond with him, cooler clothes were lent to him and the wife of one of Arabi's officers brought him good meals which she had cooked her-

[2] *Arabi Pasha*, op. cit., p. 232f.

self. The mother of the young prisoner telegraphed her thanks to Arabi.[3]

(This young midshipman grew up to be Admiral Sir Dudley de Chair who died in the summer of 1959 aged over ninety. When I saw him six months earlier his memory of this adventure was clear and he corroborated the details.)

During early September long despatches were published in the British Press about the progress of operations. There was so little pitched battle to report that much had to be comment or incidental detail. *The Times* of 8 September carried a column and a half entitled, "The War", in which it announced that the Guards Brigade under the Duke of Connaught would move to Kassassin on the following Sunday to make a feint of passing by the Egyptian army. In the opinion of their correspondent the only satisfactory strategy would be to seize the main army of the enemy and shake it to pieces.

The writer's views on Arabi's followers are interesting:

"The character of the people with whom we have to deal, will not be understood unless it is looked at from more than one point of view. It is true that, even in superior numbers, the soldiers of Arabi have failed to hold their own against English troops, but it would be unfair and untrue to accuse them of want of courage. They show lack of confidence in their power as a military body, and not without reason, but individual instances of courage are by no means unusual. The Arab who the night before last was daring enough to attempt to spike a gun in our batteries at Ramleh, showed uncommon audacity, and the cool courage with which the murderer of Messrs. Dobson and Richardson met his fate shows that the elements of heroism are not wanting in the character of the Egyptians."

The difficulty of wheeled transport in the desert had to be overcome, even in nineteenth century warfare. The wheels of the forage-carts and store wagons were found to sink deeply into the sand of the desert. Flanges were therefore fixed on each side of the tyres, making the wheels at least six inches broad.

Apart from such detailed reporting, which bears a factual imprint, the wildest tales were circulated among some war correspondents.

[3] See *How We Defended Arabi*, Broadley, p. 302 and *La Genèse de l'Esprit Nationale d'Egypte*, Sabry, p. 282.

It was said—and in some Egyptian quarters, firmly believed—that the English had brought 2,000 bloodhounds with them which, at any moment now, were to be released in pursuit of Arabi's army. Two Italian newspapers confirmed this tale. Months later (in *The Times* of 23 December) this paragraph was reproduced, from the Bombay Gazette:

"The members of the Bombay Hunt have much to answer for. They have been unconsciously the cause of serious allegations being brought against their gallant countrymen in Egypt. At a critical moment of the struggle, when men's minds were highly strung and their imaginations excited to a feverish pitch, they insisted on having a pack of hounds sent through the Canal en route to Bombay." The paragraph then goes on to say that it was the French who started the rumour in this connection, for only a Frenchman could have mistaken a foxhound for a bloodhound. The Egyptian version of the affair stated that "a ship filled with a cargo of hunting dogs had passed through the Canal to Ismailia to act as scouts for the English soldiers when they go out to fight. We conclude" wrote the Egyptian reporter, "from their now having recourse to dogs, that the climax of their ill-success and of their defeat, has come."

On the subject of war correspondents, Jean Ninet mentions some curious types. The reporter of *Temps* lost his hat while galloping on his donkey, and had the unfortunate idea of replacing it by the headgear of an English soldier, found on the battlefield. Some British officers, struck by the difference between his military cap and civilian clothes, took him to be a spy, and as he could not well express himself in English, they thought it only wise to take him prisoner. "Among this tribe of the roving pen, were to be found some of the most curious silhouettes in the world," wrote Ninet, "in get-ups borrowed from all the wardrobes of eccentric bad taste. These 'farouches', I must admit, were not English. One of them, attached to the *New York Herald*, the paper of the celebrated James Gordon Bennett, was in the fancy dress of 'grand veneur d'opera-comique'. In monumental boots, with a postillion's whip, he only lacked calf-muscles and some dogs. . . . One journal, of Liverpool or Manchester, was represented by a dentist who had lacked clientèle, but was decently dressed."

One enterprising Englishman went out on his own initiative to see, as he puts it, "something of the stirring events now taking place on the banks of the Nile." His two great requisites were horses, and a servant who could speak Arabic. He was told that neither existed, but by dint of perseverance and *backshish* he eventually procured both. He proceeded to try out the horse which seemed inclined only to stand still and kick, but a few smart strokes of his cane brought the animal to its senses and off they went at a gallop over the slippery flags with which the Alexandria streets were paved. They had not gone fifty yards before they rolled over on the hard stones. The animal was recaptured and bought. He next found a Greek who could speak English and Italian as well as Arabic and who had a muscular frame, the clothes he stood up in and no character. This writer lived to furnish *The Times* of 8 September with two and a half columns of his very entertaining experiences.

By now Arabi had decided to withdraw to Tel al Kebir, west of Ismailia, and make that the strong point to defend. It is clear from reading accounts of these days, that Arabi Pasha's colleagues and high command were greatly divided among themselves, both on military planning and on personal matters arising from jealousies and general bewilderment. Some were men of energy with a certain grasp of military strategy, but others, notably Arabi himself, relied on people who turned out to be unreliable. There were various Bedouin who trimmed their sails neatly to the prevailing wind and, at the crucial moment, a few of the men closest to Arabi deserted him. He had spent weeks of energy trying to discipline and drill his men, but by mid-August his courage seemed to be ebbing and a marked lassitude replaced it.

Old Ninet tells how he heard Arabi murmuring repeatedly to himself, "They are children—they are children, who have not yet learned to walk."

This motley mob of peasants spent much of the hot summer nights in listening to the recitation of the Koran, in dedicating their cannon to local holy worthies, in prayer and "zikr" (a religious exercise which consists in saying the name of God, with movements of the body, repeated so rapidly and often that the devotee sometimes loses consciousness). In between this, being Egyptian fellaheen, they would be sure to have been squatting round in a circle telling jokes and stories, received with roars of laughter. The first half of the night of 12 September passed as many others had done but by the dawn of the 13th the scene was drastically changed.

What happened can be seen through the eyes of a non-commissioned officer of the 42nd Highlanders who got hold of pen, ink and paper, and proceeded to write to his friends in Edinburgh: "I am happy I am now able to get an opportunity of scribbling a few lines, although I am lying here under the burning sun. Lying flat on the ground is not an easy position to write in at the best of times, but the heat of the sun and thousands of flies tormenting you makes it a thousand times worse. Now time flies slowly in the field. When I wrote to you last we were just about to disembark at Ismailia. We did so and marched eight miles through the desert, then lay down and tried to sleep till morning. We were very tired as it was horrible marching in the soft sand. . . .

"We all lay next day in the blistering heat till 4 p.m. and then marched again nine miles, and then eight miles again next morning into Kassassin, where Sir G. Wolseley was with all the rest of the army waiting on us. I cannot give days or dates, as you forget all the like of that in the field. Sir Garnet's camp was four miles long and, I think there were about 20,000 men, 14,000 horses, 60 cannons and carts and trains and boats innumerable. . . . We had tents served out on the third day and we all got served out with some biscuits and our bottles full of water. But no word of what we were to do. We fell in on parades in fighting order—that is the kilt, serge, brown helmet, waist belt, three ball bags, water bottle and haversack, and 100 rounds a man of ammunition. . . .

"We struck camp when it got dark and lit fires, and left our sick men to keep them burning to deceive the enemy, as we were now told we were to surprise him in his entrenchments. After waiting on parade about an hour, the whole Highland Brigade moved across the plain. . . . The order was spare none of the enemy, bayonet everyone of them as they would shoot us treacherously if we passed them. We were told not a shot was to be fired, to rush over the ditches and earthworks and bayonet them before the alarm could be properly given. Alas! We were deceived to our sorrow. Arabi was not to be caught asleep. His cavalry outposts had seen our advance four hours before, and every man was at his post. . . . On our left came the other Highland Regiments. The Guards, etc., were—I don't know where; anyhow they did nothing. The day was just dawning when we mounted on a bit of rising ground and we saw, 100 yards to our front, his redoubtable fortress. . . . We saw we were seen but we still thought to take them before they could man their guns. We fixed our bayonets and the sergeants their swords, and in about six seconds after the first two shots were fired

Arabi's artillery on the right and left front, and every direction, opened at once, and the blaze of rifles was horrible. We were ordered to lie down which we did. After the short run of fifty yards we were all out of breath with the excitement, and weight of our ammunition which was very great. We lay about five or ten seconds as the foe could not see us and his fire was high.

"Then the men charged, by no word of command, for none could be heard. The cheer that was given was terrific. The 42nd charged over the other fifty yards like tigers, sprang into the trenches while the bullets were whirring, whizzing and pinging like as many bees when they are casting. There is no use trying to describe it, because it is simply indescribable. . . . The pipes struck up. . . . The first man who fell, was a man of my section who was hit in the chest. He threw his rifle in the air and fell back without a groan, quite dead. . . . Over a dozen of our men fell in the attempt but at last we got a footing on the top. Sergeant-Major McNeil, Lieutenant Duff, and Lord Kennedy, myself and two men mounted and stood calling on our men! And the rest of us calling, 'Come on, the gallant Black Watch!' Then we leapt down into the fort and I fired the first shot, for we took the trenches at the point of the bayonet. It was at an officer who was leading on his men at us that I shot, and killed him.

"My ball-pouch was struck, bursting four rounds of ammunition which were in it, and burning me slightly. Almost at the same time a 79th man was struck in front of me, his brains being blown all over me. 'This will never do', said Lord Kennedy, who was with me; 'C Company, follow me', and off we all went. . . . Our artillerymen and cavalry which followed us had filled in part of the trench and now came galloping up into the fort. We gave them a deafening cheer which they returned, galloped in front of us, wheeled about the guns, and poured grapeshot and shell after the now retreating army, we ourselves picking them off like rabbits.

". . .All the Egyptian officers who were shot had a great many valuables about them, which were partly pillage from Alexandria and other places. I took their revolvers and shot them empty at the enemy, and then threw them away, as they were too heavy and we had too much work to do. . . . At the station we saw numerous engines trying to get away, but our artillery were after them at the gallop, and fired a few shells, hitting one train, which was full of ammunition which blew up in the air. . . .

"The Canal was full of dead and dying horses, camels and men.

Confusion reigned everywhere. . . . I had plenty of swords, but too many to carry, so threw them away again. We spared none, but lots made their escape. The day was won long ere then. It appeared to me to be about a week since the attack, when it was only 4 p.m. We then formed up and marched on to a train, and set off for Zaga-zig. . . .[4]

"We remained at the station till the afternoon, then took the train again to Cairo to capture Arabi himself. . ."[5]

When the news of the victory of Tel al Kebir was telegraphed to Europe, the French Minister of Foreign Affairs lost no time in expressing his satisfaction on two scores. Firstly, on account of his friendly feeling towards England, and secondly, "because her victory over the Arabs in Egypt would bear good fruit for France in Tunis and Algiers".

In thanking the French Foreign Minister for his congratulations Her Majesty's Government trusted that the event would "be followed by an early solution of the Egyptian difficulty".

During that kaleidoscopic summer of 1882 the scene was set for tragedy, though across the stage at intervals would gallivant the oddest clowns, to pass almost at once into the wings, and there to be forgotten. There was one scene, however, where the stage was held by pathos and by irony, alone.

On a June morning, Edward Henry Palmer, Professor of Arabic, set forth from his home in Mecklenburgh Square to breakfast by invitation with Lord Northbrook, First Lord of the Admiralty. The subject discussed at the meal was how the Bedouin tribes of Sinai could be induced to rally to the British when armed intervention took place in Egypt, rather than side with Arabi. By the end of the meal Palmer had virtually decided that he himself should undertake this task. He knew the Sinai desert well and knew many of the Bedouin there.

Great secrecy attended the mission. There has been much talk of whether Palmer's mission was a project of plain bribery or not. It is a legalistic point on which hairs could be indefinitely split. Certainly, much of the large sums of money made available to him were for the purchase of camels for the coming military operation.

[4] This letter was published in the *Edinburgh Daily Review*.
[5] See Parliamentary Papers, Egypt, 18, Nos. 133, 134.

But Sir Beauchamp Seymour telegraphed to the Admiralty on 6 August: "Palmer,. . .if precisely instructed as to services required of Bedouin, and furnished with funds, believes he could buy the allegiance of 50,000 at a cost of £20,000 to £30,000." £20,000 was brought to Suez on a gunboat and given to Admiral Hewett for Palmer's use.

The journal he kept on this tour was written purely for his wife, and it is only fair to remember this as one reads it.

"It seems ages since I heard anything of you all. . . .When I get into camp I am too tired after riding for nine hours and sitting for three in a little tent at noon with the thermometer at 130° in the shade. . . . I think I am the only European who ever made such a journey in midsummer. Even the Arabs are knocked up, but I keep quite well. . . . It is wonderful, though, how I get on with them—I have got hold of some of the very men whom Arabi Pasha has been trying to get over to his side and when they are wanted I can have every Bedouin at my call from Suez to Gaza. . . .

"I have already done the most difficult part of my task, and as soon as I get the precise instructions the thing is done, and a thing which Arabi Pasha failed to do, and on which the safety of the road to India depends. It has cost me some anxious moments to break the subject, and I do not mind saying, now that I am in comparative safety, that I have had a most dangerous task. . . . The bedouins keep quite quiet and will not join Arabi, but will wait for me to give them the word what to do. They look upon Abdullah Effendi—which is what they call me—as a very grand personage indeed!

"I have got the man who supplies the pilgrims with camels on my side too, and as I have promised my big sheikh £500 for himself, he will do anything for me. . . .

"You may fancy me in Arab dress on the back of a camel riding along in the moonlight over a broad, sandy plain, with a lot of ragged, cut-throat looking ruffians—yet I am quite safe with them. I have made them respect me by always insisting on having my own way, and never letting them see that I had the least fear of anything or anybody. I do not really think there are many men who would have made the journey I have done. . . .

"I have been asked to go to the coast and cut the telegraph wires and burn the poles on the Desert line, so as to cut off Arabi's communications with Turkey."

Walter Besant in his Life of E. H. Palmer (from which the above quotations are taken) publishes part of a private letter to a friend, written by Palmer on 22 July from the Wadi Mughara desert. "This business has its anxieties, but I feel quite calm about it, only it is necessary to keep one's head clear, as you can imagine. . . . I have thus far succeeded in my preliminary run through the desert beyond my wildest hopes, but it was often risky opening the game. For instance, when I made certain propositions to the big boss of these parts, he replied sententiously, 'Ahmed Pasha Arabi is with the Moslems— you belong to our enemies', and would not for some time vouchsafe another word. They tried to bustle me one day— about forty Arabs rode up to me while I was halting at mid-day, brought their camels to a stand-still on their knees, with one simultaneous motion, and then jumped off and ran to me. But I spotted my friend the sheikh whom I had seen before, and simply addressed him by name and asked him to sit down and smoke a cigarette, which he did. It was a pretty 'blow of eye' but I don't think I even let them see that it interested me. What a game it all is. How I long for the cool smoking room of the Saville, and the cooler drinks."

On 8 August, Professor Palmer left Suez for the second half of his expedition, taking with him three bags of £1,000 each in English sovereigns and a dozen regulation naval swords as presents for the sheikhs. The party consisted of himself, Captain W. Gill, R.E., a Syrian-Christian dragoman, Lieutenant Harold Charrington, R. N., Bakhor, a Jewish cook from Gaza, and two Bedouin. More Bedouin joined them later. What happened in the course of the next few days was, in part, unravelled months later by Colonel Warren (later Major General Sir Charles Warren), who was in charge of investigations and who captured and interrogated as many concerned as possible. It is a most involved tale of treachery, cupidity, misunderstanding, and stupidity. The presence of so much gold in the barren wastes of Sinai was undoubtedly the main cause of the tragedy. The party were set upon, taken prisoners, and stripped. The five men were driven in front of their Bedouin captors for about a mile to the ravine of Wadi Sadr. A Bedouin to despatch them was placed behind each, as they were made to stand in a row on the edge of the gulley. All were shot and killed at the top of the cliff or as they leapt down the side of the sixty foot precipice, in a vain endeavour to escape.

Colonel Warren found some torn scraps of paper lying about the

Wadi Sadr when he went to examine the spot. On one was written: "Found them very grasping and covetous as before, but as I could not leave any in bad humour, or play one off against another, as I did when merely exploring, I had to give so many presents in token of the right of my proposals, and pay so extravagantly for escorts, that it has nearly exhausted the funds placed at my disposal."

In November 1883, Major (afterwards Lord) Kitchener left for a survey tour of Sinai. In his report of the journey he includes the following: "I obtained from an Arab of the Haiwat tribe a story of the murder which I have never seen published in any account of it. I give it merely for what it is worth: Arabs, as everybody knows who has had to do with them, have a remarkable facility of making up a story to meet a supposed occasion.

"This was the story in the Arab's own words:—Arabi Pasha, directed by the Evil One—may he never rest in peace!—sent to his Lordship the Governor of Nakhl in Sinai, to tell him that he had utterly destroyed all the Christian ships of war at Alexandria and Suez; also that he had destroyed their houses in the same places, and that the Governor of Nakhl was to take care if he saw any Christians running about in his country, like rats with no holes, that the Arabs were to finish them at once. On hearing the news a party of Arabs started to loot Ayun Musa and Suez. Coming down Wadi Sadr they met the great Sheikh Abdullah and his party, they thought they were the Christians spoken of by Arabi Pasha, running away, so they surrounded them in the Wadi, all night they stopped round them, but did not dare to take them till just at dawn, when they made a rush on them at every side and seized them all.

"The Arab Sheikh who had come with the party ran away with the money. The Arabs did not know Sheikh Abdullah, and did not believe his statement, and when he offered money, his own Sheikh would not give it, so that they believed that the party were running away from Suez, and they finished them there. Afterwards the Great Colonel came and caught them, and they were finished at Zagazig. May their graves be defiled!" [6]

Anyone who cares to wander in the Crypt of St. Paul's Cathedral, can read on the wall:

"In memory of three brave men, Professor Edward Henry Palmer, Fellow of St. John's College, Cambridge, Lord Almoner's Reader in Arabic and a scholar and linguist of rare genius; Captain William

[6] Palestine Exploration Fund Quarterly Statement, October 1884, p. 202.

John Gill, R.E., an ardent and accomplished soldier and a distinguished explorer; Lieutenant Harold Charrington, R. N., of H. M. S. 'Euryalus,' a young officer of high promise. Who when travelling on public duty into the Sinai Desert were treacherously and cruelly slain in the Wadi Sadr, August 11th MDCCCLXXXIII. This tablet has been erected by the country in whose service they perished, to commemorate their names, their worth and their fate. That tragic fate was shared by two faithful attendants, the Syrian Khalil Atik and the Hebrew Bakhor Hassun, whose remains lie with theirs."

PART III

AFTER THE CURTAIN — 1883-1911

CHAPTER XIII

PAGEANTRY AND PRISONS

MANY rumours were current at the time as to Arabi's whereabouts and his fate after the battle of Tel al Kebir. Mr. Wilfrid Blunt gives the story as he heard it many times over, from the lips of Arabi's body-servant, Mohammed, who was with his master on the night of the battle, and who entered Wilfred Blunt's service in 1888. According to Mohammed, Arabi was in camp a mile and a half in the rear of the troops and, suspecting nothing, was sleeping soundly. It was the noise of the guns that woke him. Quickly mounting his horse he rode with his servant towards the firing, but they shortly met a crowd of fugitives who told them that there was no further hope. The scene of confusion was completed by mounted Bedouin galloping in every direction.

Arabi tried to rally whom he could, and advance, but his man-servant pleaded with him to fly with the rest, and this prayer, plus force of circumstances, prevailed. Some Bedouin of the Western Fayoum had sent Arabi good horses so he and his servant being well mounted were just able to keep ahead of the advancing English. They made for Bilbeis and from there took the train to Cairo. Arabi's own memoirs, given verbally to Mr. Blunt, only add that he said his prayers in camp before riding forth with his servant.

At a hurried meeting in Arabi's house it was decided to surrender Cairo without defence. Jean Ninet was with them and they asked him how this should be implemented. His advice was that they should go to the British General and give up their swords to him as prisoners of war and the honour of England would be engaged for their protection. They drove straight to Abassia to do this.

The scenes in Cairo included much jollification on the defeat of Arabi. Many Egyptian waverers now rushed to register themselves on the side of success, each in his various way. Some hung coloured lights outside their shops, others placed enlarged photos of the Khedive Tewfik in central positions of their establishments. Cheering crowds gathered outside Abdin Palace. Inside the Palace, with hundreds of others on 15 September, was *The Times* correspondent in Egypt who cabled his paper: "The Khedive at least was not deceived. As I congratulated him with some malice, on the loyalty of his population, he said: 'Yes, and a month ago they would have cheered as heartily if I had been the prisoner'." The Khedive gave a banquet to the heads of the British armed forces, at the Gezira Palace.

The next event was a full-scale military review in Abdin Square. Heavy cavalry, Highland regiments, Indian horsemen, Sappers from Madras, red-coated Englishmen and a Naval Brigade passed with banners aloft and bands in full play. A stand had been erected in front of Abdin Palace. Here were gathered the Khedive and his ministers, wearing their newly acquired British orders. Stars of India and Orders of St. Michael and St. George glimmered upon them, whereas the Sash of the Osmania enhanced the uniform of Sir Beauchamp Seymour. In front of this stand was a Union Jack near which Sir Garnet Wolseley, on a bay charger, took the salute. Representatives of many European countries were there and the 500 other chosen guests were mostly European.

The pomp and circumstance of Whitehall in its own setting, where the seed was sown in centuries past and has rooted and branched, is a sincere and fine thing. But surely scenes of pageantry such as this was, in the ancient capital of Egypt, must have struck a false note in many an Egyptian whose heart had genuinely stirred in response to Arabi's call. Could such a scene ever have laid foundations for a creative relationship between the two peoples, in the immediate or even the distant future? And the bestowal of noble English orders under such circumstances in such a setting, must have struck even the recipients as somewhat farcical. "Tewfik in state witnesses a review of 18,000 British troops who have re-placed him on the throne," reported *The Times*, "while Arabi from his prison window in the same square, is watching the defile of the army which scattered to the winds. in twenty minutes, his ambitious labour of a year." (The "prison window" touch enraged Jean Ninet, when he read it. He felt sure that Arabi's cell was so situated that he could no more see the review "than he could see Mount Ararat or St. Paul's".)

"To those who could appreciate the symbolic significance of that varied host, it must have conveyed a vivid idea of the extent and stability of the British Empire," continued *The Times* of 2 October. "If the native mind did not fully grasp the meaning of the pageant, it must at least have been impressed up to the limit of its capacity with the forces actually before it." Another Englishman who witnessed the scene wrote thus: "God knows what the Egyptians felt"—a briefer and perhaps a more truthful comment.[1]

By the end of October Jean Ninet had arrived in England where he had come in an endeavour to help Arabi by giving evidence in his favour. The old Swiss had undergone strenuous adventures since Arabi's defeat and arrest. He had at first been allowed to move about freely in Cairo which he had done without hesitation and was even invited by some English officers to join them at meals in their hotel.

His position was known to many of them and none denied his courage. When he had thrown in his lot with Arabi, he had already known and loved the Egyptian people for long; he had watched the growth of the national idea from its beginning and was convinced that Arabi represented something that could have been the salvation of the country and the regeneration of her masses. In Ninet's opinion a quarrel was forced upon Arabi by European diplomacy. Arabi had found himself obliged to fight the English and in his misfortune Ninet had not deserted him. Being too old for active service he had worked in Arabi's ambulance corps. It never occurred to him that after the defeat he was still in danger.

One day, as he was crossing the Ezbekiah Square, a well dressed Turkish Egyptian official sprang out of a passing carriage and arrested him. Ninet protested that as he was a Swiss citizen and when in Egypt was under French protection he should be taken to the French Consulate. The official said he knew nothing of French authority and they drove on to the Cairo Prefecture. There he was received by the Governor, a man who had supported Arabi initially but was now in the process of turning his coat. When asked by Ninet, on what warrant the arrest was made, he replied: "We have no time for warrants," and sent off Ninet to prison. There he found many of his old friends ("the best society in Cairo," he styled it). They asked him why he had been arrested—a question he was unable to answer. They too were in the same plight. One prisoner, especially, came forward and shook him warmly by the hand. It was Sheikh Mohammed Abdu.

There were wounded officers in this prison and as no doctor came for the first week, they were treated by Ninet as best he could. He succeeded in getting a message to Sir Garnet Wolseley himself,

[1] *An Englishman's Recollections of Egypt*, Baron de Kusel, Bodley Head, 1915, p. 227.

describing the state of things, which resulted in an Egyptian regimental doctor being sent. A further complaint led to some rather half-hearted cleaning up of the place, insufficient to dismay the multitude of bugs. One day, however, fifty to sixty men descended with whitewash, scrubbing brushes and chloride of lime. This heralded a visit of inspection by the Duke of Connaught. Ninet, in a somewhat ironic frame of mind, comments in his book that they might have spared themselves the effort as the Duke came no further than the courtyard.

On the twelfth day they were told that a commission of enquiry would sit upon their case and examine them. Ninet, perhaps rashly, advised his fellow-prisoners to withhold their evidence. In consequence of this, no doubt, he was removed on the day before the examination was to be held. A Circassian came to where he was lying and said in Turkish-Arabic, "Goum, ya dayous" (Get up you pig). He was ill with fever at the time and wet through with perspiration but was not allowed to change his clothes. He was passed down to two soldiers in the yard who put him in thumb screws. These thumb screws were commonly used in Egypt, not always as a torture, but it depended on the humanity of those in charge. In this case the soldiers used him kindly, being fellaheen and knowing who he was. He was taken in a carriage to his lodging and allowed to speak to his landlady from the window. She, seeing him in this pitiable state, wept as she sent down the two pieces of baggage he had left with her.

From there he was taken to the railway station and boarded a train for Alexandria. The same soldiers were with him and in the carriage they undid the screws altogether, bidding him only keep his hands hidden, so that he might not be seen to be free. Nor did they put them on again at Alexandria as he feared they might for it was dark when they arrived.

At Alexandria the Governor, a Circassian, ordered him off with a few round oaths, to the Burgo, an old fortress built into the sea. Here the conditions were far worse than in Cairo. A few loopholes gave the only light and damp dripped from the walls. In a space fit for 150 persons, lay or rather squatted 310 persons, in a state of filth and misery. Many of them were in chains, and in the morning Ninet recognised not a few old acquaintances. Some could talk French and English and nearly all were respectable men. They were very kind to him and gave him a share of their squat-

ting room. Here he remained four days, living principally on bread
and grapes shared with him by the other prisoners whose friends
had sent them this food. The night of his arrival he was visited and
closely searched. The authorities took some of his papers but
fortunately let drop his passport which a fellow-prisoner picked
up and secretly returned to him.

After some days he was again called for by the Governor and told
that a mistake has been made and that he was to go at once on board
a ship which was about to sail. Ninet asked the name of the ship
and where she was bound, only to be told that they did not know.
At the custom house he was asked whether he had a passport, but
he did not answer, fearing it would be taken from him again.
The chief official said: "You are an Ottoman subject. We have it
from the British authority," and he drew out a passport for him
in Arabic and French. He was sent on board the Dakhalia, an
Egyptian Government steamer, where he was given a deck passage
with seaman's allowance.

Here he learned for the first time that his destination was Smyrna
and Constantinople, and felt sure that he was on a fair road to some
new place of oblivion under Ottoman rule. But the worst did not
happen. His luck veered to a favourable quarter. He was able to
make friends with a ship's officer—an Armenian—who promised
to help in whatever way he could. When the ship put in at the Pira-
eus, the Armenian at risk to himself, was able to smuggle Jean
Ninet ashore. A French ship, the Amérique, was in the harbour,
and risking no further delay, he claimed a passage in her, producing
his true passport which he had all along kept hidden in his belt.
A few days later he was in Berne.[2]

Arabi, unlike Ninet, being at first under the surveillance of the
British army, was there treated with kindness and consideration
which he made a point of acknowledging. Some of the British
public, however, expressed themselves a trifle ferociously. An article
in *The Times* of 9 October debated ways and means of following up
the victory in Egypt. ". . .How then shall we convince them of our
power, teach them to believe that we have the force, a force that
we will use, and only use, if driven to extremities?" This was the
question. The suggested answers were numerous—that Arabi
should be taken in chains through every province in Egypt; that

[2] The above account is taken from a letter by Jean Ninet in *The Times* of 25
October, 1882.

leading men from each village should be brought to Cairo and allowed freely to see him in chains; the most merciful would have him to stump the country on the Khedival platform at the price of his life; the more bitter felt that nothing but public execution of the twelve ringleaders in twelve different towns would have the desired effect. If banishment were to be his fate a gross error would have been committed if he was not exiled before trial. Once tried, any penalty short of death would give him all the prestige of an acquittal, it was thought.

Yet many held very different opinions and an Egyptian Prisoners' Defence Fund was opened by Mr. Wilfrid Blunt who was determined that Arabi should have the advantages of being defended by an English barrister. One list of subscribers to this fund (published in *The Times*, 5 December 1882) included: "General C. E. Gordon (Pasha), £10; General Lord Mark Kerr, £10.10; Mr. A. W. Kinglake, £5; Mr. Spencer Charrington, £10.10; Lord Elcho, £20."

The efforts of Wilfrid Blunt and others succeeded, and on 18 October Mr. A. M. Broadley, Barrister-at-Law of Lincoln's Inn, set foot on Egyptian soil in order to stand for Arabi's defence. His legal assistant was the Hon. Mark Napier. On the journey to Alexandria Mr. Broadley had stopped in Malta, where he had heard a variety of opinions on Arabi's coming trial, from all and sundry. One portly old shopkeeper expressed a hearty wish that the Egyptians had held out longer, for then he would have had many more opportunities of selling tobacco to the British troops as they went out, and filigree work and lace as they returned home. His politics were of the practical brand.

The centre of Alexandria still lay in ruins but one or two novel features had arisen among the devastation, to whit, the Prince of Wales Grog Shop, the American Bar, the British Tar, the Tel al Kebir and the Wolseley Arms; and a French lady of determined character had installed herself in a *Grand Café* right across the pavement and refused to move until handsomely paid to do so.

Once in the train for Cairo, Mr. Broadley settled down to read that day's Egyptian Gazette and to catch up on any important new telegrams it might contain. What he did catch up on, was the feelings of some of the English residents in Egypt. "Sir," he read in the paper, "I cannot refrain from writing a few lines to express my firm opinion that there will be a miscarriage of justice if English counsel and lawyers be allowed to defend the arch-

rebel Arabi. The forensic astuteness of the members of the English
bar is such that they can logically make black appear white and
vice versa, and require other lawyers equally versed in the quibbles
of the law to convince the judge and jury of the reality of the colour
in dispute. . ." etc., etc. But Mr. Broadley was luckily made of a
resilient substance and continued his journey relatively unperturbed,
which was just as well for difficulties innumerable were ahead of him.

The first burning question was whether he and Mr. Napier would,
in fact, be allowed to defend Arabi. Mr. Broadley in his book,
How We defended Arabi, describes the balcony of Shepheards' Hotel
full of newspaper men waiting to hear the outcome of this first
round. It did not take Broadley long to win it and on announcing it
to those assembled on Shepheard's balcony, they rose as a man and
stampeded to cable the news round the world, some on donkeys
and some on foot, some in carriages, all in haste. Donkeys were an
accepted mode of procedure in Cairo of those days. Mr. Broadley
hired the services of an ex-donkey boy, Hassan, as his general facto-
tum. Hassan had become an owner of donkeys as opposed to the
driver of one donkey, by the liberality of the Prince of Wales for
whom he had worked on a late royal visit to Cairo and whose scale
of tipping had made this possible. Naturally Hassan's best donkey
was named "Brince of Wulls". He combined a love of Arabi with
a love of the English, but did not think highly of the Khedivial party.
It was Hassan who expounded to the English lawyer where he felt
Arabi had failed, by saying that when he, Hassan, took a donkey
to the Pyramids he also thought of how to get it back again, but
Arabi had led them all up to Tel al Kebir without apparent thought
of what might follow.

On 5 October, Arabi had been removed from his first prison and
placed, with his arrested colleagues, in a rambling building which
had seen many uses having been a printing press, a hotel, and a
depot for theatrical properties. Long corridors and small rooms
giving off them made a passable prison. Other rooms were offices,
translator's quarters, and so on, in connection with the trial. A
British corporal's guard was at the main door. When Mr. Broadley
first called on his client he had to creep into his cell under a ladder
and walk delicately to avoid buckets of white-wash in a fog of dust.
The windows having to be kept shut, the heat was intense, so a grill
was being made over the door into the corridor to give some ventila-
tion. This was the first time that Broadley had seen Arabi. He

was struck by the two different expressions of his face. One was a deep frown, and a withdrawn look, but when his face lighted up in talk, his eyes became alive and his smile was gentle and welcoming. His cell was furnished with a carpet, a mattress and pillows, a mosquito net, a prayer rug, a Koran and some vessels of brass and earthenware.

In this and subsequent visits, Arabi recounted at length and in detail the doings and movements of the last months. In compiling his evidence he said that he needed papers from his house but that the prison authorities refused to let his servant Mohammed, or Arabi's grown-up son, enter his cell in order to help him remember where the papers were and to receive instructions to get them. On this point Mr. Broadley appealed to Sir Edward Malet and permission was given. This was a great relief to Arabi for although his memory was clear on nearly every point he confessed to Mr. Broadley once, "When I think of the bombardment, the old stunned feeling here [pointing to his head] seems to return and my memory becomes confused." His servant Mohammed, who had been with him throughout, could often help to clarify his thoughts.

Included in Arabi's written instructions to his counsel were details of bad treatment while in this Egyptian Government prison. He asserted that a party of the Khedive's household, among them the manager of his stables and one of his bodyguard, had burst into his cell, searched him all over, even pulling off a talisman he had worn round his neck. When Arabi said he would remove it himself, they shouted that they had been ordered to do it. Other visitors of the same type appeared later.

"Finally," said Arabi, "on the night of the 9th of October, at about 9.30 p.m. having undressed myself and lain down to sleep, I heard the door opened and a group of about ten or twelve persons came into my room; but being in total darkness I was unable to distinguish them. Suddenly one of them cried out in a loud voice, 'Eh! Arabi,—don't you know me?' Thinking that I was about to be murdered, I got up and replied, 'No, I do not'. Then I heard shouted, 'I am Ibrahim Agha,' and he swore at me, calling me a dog and a pig, and spat at me three times. I stood quite quiet, and gradually perceived that it really was Ibrahim Agha, tutungi (pipe bearer) to the Khedive."[3]

[3] *How We Defended Arabi and His Friends*, A. M. Broadley, p. 139 f. Chapman and Hall, 1884.

This eunuch had recently been involved in a case about diamonds stolen from Abdin Palace, but had managed to extricate himself. His post at court was to hand round the Turkish pipes to the guests of the Khedive at official receptions. Some of these court servants held great power, as indeed was true down to the time of Farouk. It was said that the Khedive Tewfik was so under the sway of his valet, one Fréderique by name, that he, the Khedive, was jokingly known in some Egyptian quarters, as Mademoiselle Fréderique.[4] When Mr. Broadley went to the Palace on 23 October to pay his respects to the Khedive on the occasion of the feast of Kourban Bairam, he felt embarrassed at being handed an amber-mouthed pipe by the said Irabhim Agha. Arabi himself appeared almost cheerful for the Bairam feast and asked Broadley to convey his salutations to Sir Edward Malet with an apology for not being able to do so personally, as in other years.

One thing bothered Arabi in prison. He was allowed no light to work with after dark, and he had much writing to do for his counsel. All applications were refused on the grounds that someone had been caught smuggling petrol into the prison. Arabi insisted on writing to Mr. Moberley Bell *The Times* correspondent hoping that he might show publicly that he, Arabi, had nothing to do with this affair. "You have perhaps heard," he wrote, "that my servant entered my rooms in the prison and left with me a bottle of petroleum in order that I might burn the prison. In due justice to me you ought to deny this report, for I never have been allowed to see my servant from the date when I was first brought here. [He was writing before permission to see the man had been granted.] And besides, why should I burn myself and die against the law? Had I wanted to do such a thing I could have done so when guarded by English soldiers. At the same time I must point out to you that had I despaired of my innocence being proved, I had plenty of time to have left this country and have reached a neighbouring one, or even England, the shelter of most fugitives. But I threw myself on the honour of the English in Egypt, thinking that I was as safe as in entering London."

On the door of one of the small rooms, like Arabi's, which acted as a cell, were written the words "Mohammed Abdu, journalist"; within was the Sheikh. Mr. Broadley said that he was frankly disappointed on first seeing Sheikh Mohammed Abdu. He lacked

[4] See *La Gènese de l'Esprit National d'Egypte*, M. Sabry, p. 168.

all assurance in himself or his cause. He was hesitant and dazed, not angry, or militant or stirred. He too had to report on abusive visits from servants of the Khedive's household, but prefaced his remarks by saying, "With my highest respects to the Khedive, may God preserve him". His cell was empty save for a mattress, a Koran and a brass ewer. It took Mr. Broadley some time to gain his confidence. Slowly, over the days, he became more decided in his reports and bolder in his statements. His mental and spiritual confusion must have been intense. He must have known agony of mind, for he was capable of deep suffering.

Ibrahim Agha and the other roughs had taken from him his books,—two volumes, on moral science, and the first volume of a history of the Middle Ages translated from French into Arabic. "And when I asked," Mohammed Abdu said in his report, "Where are you taking them to? Surely you are going to deliver them to my house?' he answered, 'Have you got a house?' Then I was quiet, and for eighteen days I saw neither a book nor a man, till a person belonging to the English Government came and asked how I was getting on, and I asked leave for a Koran to be brought to me, and he gave leave and I was as pleased as if I had been let out of prison."

Mohammed Abdu had to go through the bewildering and rocky desert traversed by those who wonder whether they have acted rightly or wrongly. This was spared Arabi, for he had no doubts and was still capable of anger. He showed it once in prison. Crowds used to collect outside his nailed up window. They were just visible through the Venetian blinds. There were women and children who sat on the ground and wailed at intervals on his behalf. There were silent groups of men, poor people, who felt for him. The crowds grew larger every day till the authorities were forced to disband them as they formed. This angered Arabi more than anything else during his imprisonment.

An erstwhile supporter of Arabi, who had backed out in time, from his point of view, was now appointed to be a judge at the coming trial. He had played his cards well. (He must have been hardy, for he had not only survived a banishment to the Sudan at one point in his career, but had managed to learn French, English and German while there.) Mr. Broadley records how he greeted him with a set speech in which he said, "Your presence forms an epoch in our history and must be considered as a landmark in our progress. It is the first time these several thousand years that foreign lawyers have appeared before an Egyptian court. We hail their arrival as a sign that England has determined to give us judicial reforms and better tribunals."[5] As Mr. Broadley commented, these happened to be among the hopes and aims of those he was about to judge.

Letters poured in, during these days, from different ends of the earth, with suggestions about the case. One original viewpoint was that, as Arabi's surrender had been illegal, he was still technically in British custody, and consequently a writ of habeas corpus should be obtained from the High Court of Justice against either Sir Garnet Wolseley or Sir Edward Malet. Mr. Bernard, special correspondent in Cairo for *The New York Herald*, also had an imaginative scheme. It was that the financial magnates behind his paper should buy Arabi outright, £25,000 was the price mentioned. Arabi would then write three-quarters of a column every week for a year, on Egyptian politics, receiving a fair wage for doing so.

As well as these sorts of communications, which Arabi's legal advisers could afford to treat lightly, they were grappling with complicated negotiations in Cairo and back and forth from London, under the heading, Rules of Procedure. A compromise plan was at last reached which made the outcome of the trial a foregone conclusion. Arabi and six of his colleagues were to plead guilty to the accusation of rebellion, the death sentence was to be passed but this was to be immediately commuted to banishment from Egypt. Their property would be confiscated, but not the property of their wives. All charges against Arabi for having been responsible for the looting and burning of Alexandria were to be dropped, for the evidence produced had been too nebulous.

When Arabi heard of this arrangement he was not too pleased. He had confidence that his counsel and his friends in England had thought this plan to be the most advantageous possible, but, as he explained to Broadley, he would have preferred considerable discussion in public, for he had hoped that the light thus shed on the situation of Egypt in general would have helped to bring about the reforms which he had failed to achieve, owing to military defeat. He found pleading to rebellion a hard pill to swallow. But, as Mr. Broadley pointed out, Arabi had agreed that his fate depended on England, and as England had just expended herself in money and men to crush him as a rebel, he could hardly expect English support

[5] *How We Defended Arabi*, op. cit., p. 156.

for a plan in which he was not called a rebel. For in that case, a simple process of logic would have convicted England of having taken, at best an unnecessary and at worst, a wrong course of action.

Arabi accepted this reasoning, and by the end of November the scene was set for the pre-ordained verdict to be officially given.

CHAPTER XIV

TO THE PARADISE OF ADAM

ARABI's trial was fixed for Sunday, 3 December, at 8.0 a.m. As the time had been arranged at the last minute, many journalists and would-be spectators were caught unawares. Even the Scotsman on sentry duty only suspected something of the sort on the morning itself. So when Messrs. Broadley and Napier arrived at the prison, the sentry's hopes rose and he eagerly asked them if his duties were nearly over, and what chances there were of his getting home by Christmas, which naturally, for him, was the focal point of the proceedings.

The room where the judgment would be pronounced was in the prison building. One judge had arrived before the counsels for the defence. They found him busying around as he waved various servants hither and thither with orders to dust chairs, distribute blotting paper, and generally prepare the scene. It might well have been preparations for the opening act of a comic opera, for the busy-body judge was in a uniform which carried a maximum of gold lace to the square foot, and as he darted here and there, a long Turkish sword swung at his side.

Soon the newspaper correspondents began to arrive, *The Times*; *The Standard*, represented by Mr. Chirol (later Sir Valentine); the *Journal des Débats*; *The New York Herald*; *The Daily Telegraph*. A Swiss newspaper had sent a lady reporter, which was considered an unusual step. *The Illustrated London News*, *The Graphic* and the *Monde Illustré* were represented by artists rapidly sketching in a corner, for they would have but a few minutes to complete their picture once the trial began.

Some of the journalists did not realise that the proceedings and the culmination had been pre-arranged, so they settled in their places as though for several hours, with papers, pencils, note-books and other signs of office carefully organised around them. Arabi was dressed in singular fashion, military trousers, a sort of dust coat and a white silk scarf round his neck. At first he showed signs of nervousness, but soon gathered composure. The reporter for the *Observer* especially noted, with admiration, the prisoner's "dignified demeanour".

The numerous highly decorated judges took their places. The charge of rebellion was read. Arabi's short declaration was handed to them which stated that of his own free will, and by the advice of his Counsel, he pleaded guilty.

The court room was crowded for the second brief sitting which took place after an hour's adjournment. The Clerk rose and read Ahmed Arabi's condemnation to death for the crime of rebellion.

A few moments afterwards the Clerk rose again to his feet and declaimed the Khedive's pardon which commuted the penalty of death to perpetual exile from Egypt and its dependencies.

All was officially over. Some journalists crossed the room to shake Arabi by the hand. The Swiss lady reporter demanded, rather more loudly than it was necessary, a personal interview with him. Mrs. Mark Napier who had joined her husband in Egypt, had a small bunch of roses beside her with which she meant to cheer up Arabi after he had left the room, but a man sitting next to her took them from the desk by her seat and put them into Arabi's hands. Much play was made in some papers over this incident and certain untrue things were said. Mrs. Napier had done much to comfort the wives and families of the prisoners by friendly visits to their homes.

Back in his cell, Arabi spread out his rug and said his prayers. He next thanked his Counsel and then settled down to write a letter of thanks to Mr. Blunt, to whose tireless efforts he felt he owed the outcome of the trial. His thoughts were also with his fellow prisoners. On the following day he wrote officially to Mr. Broadley:

"I should not like people to suppose that I have saved my life without remembering my brothers, the officers, the ulema, and the omdahs, who are imprisoned here with me or in the different provinces of Egypt. Therefore, I pray you, request the Commission of Enquiry to allow you to be present at their interrogatories, because I declare to you there is nothing against those men, for they are guiltless of any violation of the laws of man. . . . Again I implore you to look after the fate of all my fellow prisoners.

Ahmed Arabi, the Egyptian."

He next wrote a letter to *The Times* in which he acknowledged having pleaded guilty to a charge of rebellion against the Khedive. "The English Ministers," he wrote, "have often proclaimed me to be a rebel, and I cannot expect that they will suddenly change their opinion; nor, indeed, is it possible for them to do so at the present moment.

"I shall cheerfully proceed to any place which England may be pleased to appoint for my residence, and remain there till the day comes when it will be possible for England to modify her opinion concerning me." He said that he left Egypt with perfect tranquillity and confidence in the future, knowing that England could no longer delay the reforms which he and his friends struggled for.

He expressed his opinion in this letter, that Egypt would be no more "in the hands of a myriad of foreign employees filling every available post, to the exclusion of the Egyptians; our native courts will be purified of abuses; codes of law will be enacted, and, which is more important, carried out; a Chamber of Notables will be instituted with a voice and a right of interference in the affairs of the Egyptian people; the swarm of usurers in the village will be driven out. The English people, when they see all these things, will then be able to realise the fact that my rebellion had a very strong justification.

"The son of an Egyptian fellah, I tried, to the best of my power, to secure all things for the dear country to which I belong and which I love. My ill-fortune did not allow of my carrying out these objects. I hope the English people will complete the work which I commenced. If England accomplishes this task, and thus really gives Egypt to the Egyptians, she will then make clear to the world the real aim and object of Arabi, the rebel. . . ."

The next vital question was to where Arabi and the six other officers who received the same sentence should be exiled. Many suggestions circulated. Fiji was one, but this was soon dropped. A dinner given by the American Consul-General in Cairo helped to show the disadvantages of this scheme. There was considerable sympathy for Arabi's cause in America, and an after-dinner speaker on this occasion mentioned, though jokingly, the possibility of a daring rescue of Arabi from Fiji by American schooners.

Finally it was settled that Arabi and his friends should all be sent to Ceylon. Mr. Broadley went to inform him of this, complete with atlas under his arm to indicate its whereabouts. Arabi may not have known exactly where Ceylon was but he did know something about it, for he received the news thus: "This is really too much honour; not content with simply decreeing my exile, my adversaries seem actually bent on sending me to Paradise as well. Have you never heard how when our first parents parted in the plains of Mesopotamia after being driven out of Eden, our common father went to Ceylon, since called the Paradise of Adam, while our common mother reached Hedjaz, since known as Paradise of Eve? Nothing could be more just. I am driven out of Egypt, the garden of the world,—I go to Ceylon, the Paradise of Adam; I hail it as a happy omen."

Arabi was not always cheerful however. The altered note of the Egyptian press worried him much, for papers that heretofore supported him, had no further good to say of him in his fall. He also saw parts of the English and European Press either in translation or illustration. The paper *Truth* was a favourite of his, the name especially appealed to him. Mr. Labouchere was then editor and Arabi wrote to thank him for his unbiassed views on the Egyptian question. But a cartoon in *Punch* angered him. Entitled, Arabi the Blest, it showed him smoking a cigar, with what looked like brandy and soda beside him. As he neither smoked nor drank alcohol he did not appreciate this picture.

The prison and the legal authorities were much bothered after the trial by ceaseless visits from servants, dependents and members of the prisoners' families anxiously enquiring for news of where their friends, relations and masters were to be sent, and how.

To lessen this, their quarters were moved to where a corridor in front of the rooms could be partitioned off and made into a foyer where the prisoners, under surveillance, could be in touch with their families and with each other. It was ten weeks since they had met and their greetings were full of affection.

The prisoners next concentrated on compiling lists of family, servants, in-laws and poor relations whom they hoped to be able to ship with them to Ceylon. The first long lists had to be drastically revised. In the homes, the wives and families were also compiling lists. Never having travelled before they seemed to have had but three main ideas on what to take, warm coats, sugar and coffee, none of which was absolutely necessary in Ceylon.

It was not long before a difficulty appeared which, in the eyes of the prisoners, would have been calamitous. They were told that they would make the journey in separate ships. The very thought filled them with dismay. A letter was drawn up in the form of a plea to travel together, in which came the sentence:

"and we offer our best thanks to His Highness the Khedive for his handsome treatment towards us, which we shall not forget in all time, and shall pray for his prosperity". When Arabi saw this he was disgusted and refused to sign it, pointing out that he had said, and still said, that the Khedive was unfit to rule over them, therefore to put his name to such a sentence would be tantamount to lying. Instead, he wrote a dignified statement drawing the attention of the Egyptian Government to their unanimous wish to make the voyage together to the place appointed, and saying that since it was their desire to go in company with their families, they would never think of complaining of want of accommodation in the steamer.

Mr. Broadley fought this battle for them with success, and their minds were put at rest on the point.

When the procedure of the trial and the ultimate sentences were agreed upon with the Egyptian Government, it was also agreed that Arabi and the other officers would lose their titles, honours and grades, by decree. The decree was duly issued on 24 December. But that was not considered sufficient. The following day, quite unannounced, two carriages arrived and the prisoners were ordered to get in and be driven off—where they knew not. The carriages drew up in the Kasr al Nil barracks square. Here were gathered a detachment of Egyptian soldiers, and in the next ten minutes a ridiculous little ceremony took place. The prisoners were marched in front of the troops where they were asked to deliver up their swords, decorations and all such visible signs of honour. To comply was impossible, for they had not been told what was about to take place nor given time in the prison even to tidy themselves up before being bundled into the carriages. Nothing more could be done after the demand was read but to get into the carriage and drive back to the prison. As Arabi left, the Captain of the Egyptian detachment called after him, "O Arabi, you have brought the English to Egypt!" Apart from a small crowd of Egyptian passers-by who had gathered to watch, and some press reporters, the only other person to hear this cry was Tommy Atkins who already inhabited Kasr al Nil barracks, where he was to live for the next seventy years.

The Times reporter cabled a description of the scene to his paper, in which he commented: "The prisoners will leave this evening for Suez, and with them we may hope, the fable of an Egyptian

National Party!" Not being a "fable", the "hope" could hardly be fulfilled. The correspondent, however, did not forget that it had been Christmas Day, so he included in his despatch the fact that thousands of European civilians had not passed a merry Christmas and would not begin the New Year happily, owing to the delay in settling the indemnities, or any portion of them. Mutatis mutandis.

It was late at night on 26 December, in bright moonlight, that the train drew slowly out of the siding in Kasr al Nil taking Arabi and his party to Suez on the first step of their exile. The principal figures were calm and dignified, but the send-off was not without domestic alarms and excursions. At the last moment Arabi's son's wife and her sister were missing. Rumour had it that the policeman on guard at Arabi's home had thought it his duty to prevent them leaving the house, the reason for their leaving being apparently immaterial to him. The station master was waiting impatiently, whistle in mouth, but the British Military authorities insisted on holding everything till the missing ladies eventually turned up and were safely ensconced in the compartments for the women and children and baggage.

Most of the prisoners and their families were very hard up. Arabi's sequestered property had amounted to a pittance. All day long friends had been arriving with gifts of clothing, portmanteaux, food and money.[6] So the party eventually left with a sense of sympathy and support from more quarters than one; neither did it go unappreciated by Arabi, that Major Fraser of the Kings Royal Rifle Corps who was in command of his British Military guard took a seat in the carriage next to him informally.

Three days later, on 29 December, Sheikh Mohammed Abdu received his sentence. It was exile from Egypt for three years and three months. Before Mr. Broadley left, his work accomplished, he returned to the prison one evening and there, in the dark, wished Mohammed Abdu goodbye and good luck.

Hassan, the donkey owner, was able to add two more to his stable from the proceeds of the last months, and with a due sense of justice he called the new donkeys Broadley and Napier.

The ship carrying Ahmed Arabi, the other exiles and families,

[6] See *Fortnightly Review*, November, 1883, p. 636.

steamed on through the Indian Ocean as the year 1882 disappeared below the horizon. And with it the curtain comes slowly down on the story of its events. But the lives of those two Egyptians continued—Ahmed Arabi and Mohammed Abdu.

Mohammed Abdu's exile took him to Beirut. He had a friendly and respectful welcome there but he felt his absence from Egypt acutely. He was grateful for the reception he was given but wrote to a friend, "They are not like my own people, and a day spent here is not like a day at home."[7] He became adjusted to it, however, as he made new friends and picked up threads of interest.

One day he received a letter from Paris. It was from his old professor, Sheikh Jamal al Din al Afghani asking that he would join him there and help found an Islamic society to be called the Society of the Indissoluble Link. Mohammed Abdu jumped at this invitation, for he had long wished to visit Europe. No sooner had the two friends met in Paris than they started to work in earnest on a paper for their society, called by the same name, *The Indissoluble Link*. Their aim was to arouse Moslems wherever they were to a unity and an awareness of their heritage. This is an aim which could be expressed in many ways. Jamal al Din was the political director of the paper and the tone he set was on the whole, violent and aggressive. As of yore, Mohammed Abdu caught some of the latter's anti-Western passion, bitterness and hate. But doubts soon rose in his mind about the ultimate value, or even achievements, to be gained by bitterness even with cause.

Circumstances helped him to discontinue this work, for after eight or nine months of publication, some of the views expressed in *The Indissoluble Link* had drawn the marked disapproval of English and Turkish authorities. It was forbidden entry into Egypt, India and the Sudan, and such difficulties were put in the way of publication that it had to close down, though not without a fight in which Sheikh Jamal al Din, in particular, thought of every dodge imaginable to get the paper past the censor.

Before the newspaper closed down, the two Sheikhs received friends new and old in their tiny office. One of the assistant editors was a colourful individual called Mirza Bakir. At one time in his past career he had thrown off Islam and become a Christian during which era he conducted spirited propaganda for a missionary society. But in the course of time he rebounded to Islam with renew-

[7] *Mohammed Abduh*, Translated C. Wendell, op. cit., p. 49.

ed vigour and expiated his lapse by almost embarrassing enthusiasm for the faith of his fathers. Wilfrid Blunt visited Mohammed Abdu in Paris and urged him to come to London, even offering him money for the fare. He accepted and Mirza Bakir came as interpreter, for his English was good. He had learnt the Bible by heart during his sojourn with the missionaries.

Mohammed Abdu's idea was to meet English politicians face to face and speak openly of his convictions. Mirza Bakir's idea was to leave no stone unturned in his effort to get the British Isles to embrace Islam. At one point the Sheikh had to tell him quite clearly that his ardours must be damped for the duration of this trip. But Mirza Bakir had a final trump card to play. It so happened that Queen Victoria had just received a laudatory ode from some Indian dignitaries; Her Majesty expressed a desire to have it translated into English poetry. Someone who knew of Mirza Bakir's linguistic gifts said that the very man for the work was in London at that moment. The Queen was so delighted with Mirza Bakir's poetic English rendering of the ode, that she graciously offered him a substantial sum of money for his pains. Mirza Bakir momentarily threw Mohammed Abdu's directive to the winds. He returned the money and told the Queen of his own request, that Her Majesty would oblige him by becoming a Moslem. The answer to this is not recorded in the tale.

Mohammed Abdu stayed at the Blunts' London house in James Street and was taken by Mr. Blunt to visit newspaper and political figures of the day. His presence in the Lobby of the House of Commons, dressed in white turban and blue robe, caused quite a stir. Several members were sympathetic to his cause if not always helpful in their suggestions. One told the Sheikh that the best way for the Egyptians to show their dislike of the English Occupation was for them to refuse to pay their taxes, to which the Sheikh answered that in his opinion this would be a quick way to total annexation into the British Empire.

The Pall Mall Gazette of 17 August 1884 published an interview with him. Sheikh Mohammed Abdu was outspoken. "We Egyptians of the Liberal party believed once in English liberalism and English sympathy; but we believe no longer. . . . There is no Moslem in Egypt so oppressed as to wish for any more of your help. We ask only one thing of you, and that is that you leave us at once and forever. . . . If England wanted to repair the wrong she has done to us, she would, as I have said, give us a first proof of her sincerity by ordering back her troops from Egypt."

Mohammed Abdu went on to speak of his ideas about an ideal ruler for Egypt. In many respects his remarks might have been said 6, not 66 years ago. "It is not for me to say who this ruler should be. But who ever may be chosen he should be named for a term of years, say seven or ten, at the end of which term the people should be allowed to elect their rulers finally for themselves. If he proved an honest man he might then retain office. But if dishonest, the people would have the comfort of thinking that he would not be there for ever and so would take patience.

"Any new ruler now, who should be a Moslem and should come into office as the deliverer of Egypt from the English troops, would be loved by the Egyptians. Only he must be a Moslem and if possible an Egyptian by birth. It is essential, however, that he be content with limited power. What we want is not a new king, but a chief of our Egyptian nation. . . . This kind of ruler the Egyptians understand, and they do not want a king." The Sheikh ended: "Leave us now and we will call on God to reward you as our benefactors. But do not attempt to do us any more good. Your good has done us too much harm already."

A few days later Sir William Gregory wrote to Wilfrid Blunt: "I have read with great interest Mohammed Abdu's replies to his interviewer. They are very valuable and would be ten times more so if anything could pierce the crust of our English stupidity and self-complacency. But we have made up our minds that the Egyptians whom we have been bombarding and slaughtering ought to love us, and that if they don't it is their perversity, which only time and subjection can remove."[8] Mohammed Abdu had an interview with Lord Hartington, then Minister of War, which rankled in his mind and which was reproduced with comment in *The Indissoluble Link*. (This English visit took place before the paper was discontinued.) The gist of the interview was Lord Hartington expressing his belief that the Egyptians were gratified to dwell in security under the British Government, and that ignorance was so prevalent among the masses that they did not differentiate between a foreign and an Egyptian ruler.

Undoubtedly there were men in Egypt about whom that was wholly true. But equally there were many of whom it was quite untrue.

[8] See *Gordon at Khartoum* by W. S. Blunt, Stephen Swift Ltd., 1912, p. 632.

That it seemed the only view point of Lord Hartington, stung Mohammed Abdu to answer that aversion to domination and repugnance
for such rule are among the most deeply rooted feelings in man's
nature, and are in no way dependent either on education or learning.

It was not long after the Sheikh's return to Paris that the paper,
The Indissoluble Link, was suppressed. Jamal al Din al Afghani
went off to Russia and Mohammed Abdu toured the lands of North
Africa. Before they parted Mohammed Abdu expressed his growing
conviction that forceful politics would not bring the results he
desired, and that the right sort of Moslem government depended
on more than the absence of foreigners. "It is men who will accomplish everything," he said.[9] But Jamal al Din felt this to be too slow
a means of change, and said so, as he boarded a train for Moscow.
In Tunis and the neighbouring countries, Mohammed Abdu went
from man to man, speaking of his aims, observing reactions to his
ideas, listening and talking, hearing and expounding.

Early in 1885 he returned to Beirut, hoping to live there quietly
with time to relax. But soon all and sundry sought him out, and
his house in the Burg al Haidar suburb became the meeting place
of people seeking knowledge, solace, ideas and help. There were
Christians among them as well as Moslems. At the end of the year
he was invited to teach at the Sultania School. Mohammed Abdu
was never able to resist an offer to teach. He flung himself into
the work with all his old zest, introducing new methods, tackling
administrative reform and revitalizing the outlook of students
and staff alike.

At the school celebrations for the end of the academic year, he
was sitting in his seat listening to the proceedings, when someone
asked if he would not address them extemporarily on any topic he
would like to choose. Within a few minutes he was on his feet
and he spoke for an hour on a subject which rather startled his
audience, used as they were to conventional orations of praise on
such occasions as this. His speech was entitled "The Cause of
Backwardness in the Orient". Some of the ideas expressed must
have been gripping at the time but are of even greater significance
today:

"As to the science that we feel ourselves in need of," he said,
"people think that it is industrial science and the material side of
work in agriculture and commerce, provided by it, but this is a vain

[9] See *Islam and Modernism in Egypt*, op. cit., p. 63.

supposition. For if we refer back to what every one of us complains of, we shall find something which lies beyond ignorance of industrial matters and what pertains to them. Even if industries were within our power we might find ourselves unable to maintain them; or perhaps their use would be ready to our hands, but it would escape us because of something in ourselves. What we ought to be complaining of is the weakness of our aspirations, our impotence, the disunity of our aims, and the neglect of our basic interests.

"The industrial sciences will not propel us towards the resolving of our complaints. Our science is a science beyond all these, a science that touches the soul; and this is the science of human life. The science that revitalizes the soul is the science of the discipline of the soul and all such discipline is to be found in religion. What we have forgotten is to examine the disciplines of religion."[10]

It was here, in Beirut, that Mohammed Abdu's first wife died, leaving him with a baby daughter. There was no woman in the house to help and for some time he felt quite overcome by grief, loneliness and trials. When help came and he returned to teach, his class debated before his entry how best to express their sympathy. But when the moment came, they were silent, for he greeted them and went to his seat as though nothing had happened. He announced that the lesson was to be on composition and proceeded to dictate an Arabic ode which dealt with the best way of facing personal sorrow. They were thus enabled to talk indirectly on what was uppermost in all their minds. Some time later he was married again, to the niece of his friend, the Mayor of Beirut.

During these days old Mirza Bakir turned up again, and with Mohammed Abdu, founded a society with the aim of uniting Christians, Jews and Moslems to create a force which would combat the supremacy of the West over the East. Whenever Mirza Bakir had an idea something curious would be sure to ensue, as likely as not, involving Queen Victoria. Several Englishmen joined this society, among them the Reverend Isaac Taylor who had been corresponding with Mohammed Abdu and to whom the aims of the society greatly appealed. He wrote articles on the subject and boldly addressed a gathering of fellow-clergymen, some of whom contemplated the idea with dismay. They apparently brought the scheme to the notice of Queen Victoria who contacted the Sultan

[10] *Mohammed Abduh*, translated by C. Wendell, op. cit., p. 67.

of Turkey, requesting him to deal suitably with those in his realm
who were propagating such aims.

The Sultan took action, and five of the leading spirits were ordered
out of Syria. Sheikh Mohammed Abdu and his family were conveniently about to leave anyhow. It is said that the Sultan of Turkey
took such definite and unusually rapid action in the affair for
fear that if it spread, Queen Victoria would shortly be a Moslem
and, having more powers behind her than he had, the mantle of the
Caliphate would fall on her small round shoulders, after his death.[11]
The vision of Regina Imperatrix Amira Mumineenorum was more
than he could face.

Arabi's exile was less eventful than Mohammed Abdu's, and its
eighteen years were long drawn out; but he was treated with understanding by the authorities in Ceylon, and this meant much to him.
The Governor of Ceylon, Sir James Longden, received the Egyptians
with every civility and was in close touch with the Foreign and Colonial Offices about their affairs. Arabi's wife and younger children
had stayed in Cairo as Madame Arabi was expecting a baby.
The question of her journey to Ceylon, after the baby's birth,
was the cause of much official correspondence.

Lord Granville was ready to concur with Lord Dufferin (who was
by then on a special mission to Egypt) in persuading the Egyptian
Government to give her a free passage, Sir James Longden was
ready to affirm to Lord Derby Arabi's wish that she should come.
But it was Lord Granville who realised that no one actually knew
what Madame Arabi herself desired. This vital point had been
overlooked by others, well-intentioned as they were. More despatches back and forth on this particular angle of the subject
finally brought to light the fact that Madame Arabi would much
rather stay in Egypt and live with her old mother.

A year later the subject of money arose. The Egyptian Government was asked to raise the exiles' allowance but refused and the
British Government was also averse to it. The then Governor
of Ceylon, Sir Arthur Gordon, wrote strongly in defence of the
exiles to Lord Derby, saying how they dreaded getting into debt,
yet could not live on their allowance.

"I see no signs whatever of extravagances," he wrote, "or even
comfort about the humble establishments of these exiles, quite

[11] Related by Sheikh Abdul Wahab al Najjar. See *Mohammed Abduh* by
Osman Amin, p. 105.

the reverse, and I cannot but think that the Egyptian Government would consult its own reputation were it to show somewhat more liberality towards those detained here on its behalf. I ought, I think, to add that the behaviour of Arabi and his companions during their stay in Ceylon has been exemplary. They have neither engaged in political intrigues nor assumed the attitude of martyrs, but have with great dignity and good taste, cheerfully accepted and made the best of their position, not thrusting themselves forward into notice nor on the other hand shrinking from society, and readily performing the duties which naturally fall to them as well educated members of the Mohammedan community."[12]

It is noteworthy that the only plea Arabi himself wrote, apart from those which he signed with all the others years later, was one requesting that he should not be treated financially any better than the rest of his friends in exile.

In a letter dated 14 February 1884, Sir William Gregory speaks of visiting his old friend Ahmed Arabi. "You have no idea how he is liked and respected by everyone. The colonel in command here and his wife, a clever and charming woman, think him one of the finest, most modest, and truthful men they have ever met. Mr. Campbell, the head of the police, who has a good deal to say of him (more than Arabi thinks) speaks of him in the highest possible terms. . . . I regret to say that some things take place which must mar the contentment of the exiles. They are subjected at every hour to intrusions without introductions from all the vulgar riff-raff which lands at Colombo and which go to see the large tortoise and then to see Arabi. While Lord Rosebery (whom I had introduced to Arabi) was speaking very seriously to him, a Melbourne betting bookmaker forced himself in and hailed Arabi in the most familiar manner."[13]

Another matter to which the Ministries of Foreign Affairs and of Colonies had to bend their minds and ply their pens was the state of health of Toulba, one of Arabi's fellow officers. The poor man had suffered badly from asthma and the climate of Ceylon brought on a relapse. A certificate was sent to London signed by Brigadier Surgeon White on 17 March 1883 saying that a long stay in the island might be fatal for Toulba.

[12] Parliamentary Papers, Egypt, No. 37, 1884.
[13] *Sir William Gregory, Autobiography* edited by Lady Gregory, John Murray, 1894, p. 392.

On 9 May, Sir Julian Pauncefote of the Foreign Office wrote to Mr. Herbert of the Colonial Office, requesting him to "move the Earl of Derby to cause Lord Granville to be informed what steps his Lordship considers it advisable to take in the matter".

Toulba petitioned to be sent to Beirut; the British Government suggested he should go to Penang. The asthma seemed genuine enough, but behind the lengthy official correspondence on the subject, is the Egyptian's evident longing to smell once more the lands of the Eastern Mediterranean. Toulba telegraphed "Like Syria, Cyprus, Tunis." He was offered the Cape of Good Hope. He declined. It was finally suggested that he remove himself to another part of Ceylon.

* Information on which the first part of this chapter is based comes from *How We Defended Arabi* by A. M. Broadley, Chapman Hall, 1884.

CHAPTER XV

OF FAR GREATER CONSEQUENCE

IN the meantime Sheikh Mohammed Abdu had received a pardon, largely through British influence in Egypt, and had returned to his native land. His desire was to teach again but he found, to his consternation, that all teaching posts were closed to him by the Khedive Tewfik for fear of what effect he might have on the rising generation of Egyptians. Instead, he was offered a judgeship and accepted it, though he felt it was not his true role. Yet it was not long before he found ample opportunity in this work for his special gifts and ideas. What he had learnt in his teaching days, and his intuition into the minds and motives of men, held him in good stead.

He would bring to light unusual angles on the case in hand and was not afraid to change his own mind as he went. A framework of guilt that he had pieced together during the trial would sometimes collapse in the light of one fact which he had uncovered at the end of the proceeding. He always impressed upon his law students that it was better to achieve a reconciliation of litigants than to produce a clever judgment.

In court he had a habit of pushing his turban forward on his head when he believed a man to be guilty and of tilting it backwards if the man seemed to him innocent. A prisoner once beseeched him from the dock not to do this, as he felt himself quite unable to tell the truth while watching anxiously for this sign.

It was during these years that Mohammed Abdu decided to learn French. His teacher must have found him an unusual pupil. At the first lesson he announced that he would have no time to begin but only to finish, and that he had also decided on the method he would follow. This was to read aloud, as best he could, from a novel of Dumas and the teacher had to correct his pronunciation and tell him the meaning of the words. Grammar and syntax were to be absorbed as automatic by-products. One of the reasons he gave for the necessity of acquiring French, was that the interests of Europe and the Islamic states were now so mingled that every one should be able to imbibe what good Europe had to offer and, at the same time, learn what was evil in its ways and eschew it.

Mohammed Abdu's life was exceedingly full, for he was appointed to the Legislative Council, to the Committee of Administration of Al Azhar and in June 1899 he was made Grand Mufti of Egypt, the highest legal post he could hold. In addition to this he was still lecturing at Al Azhar where one year his lectures were attended by the great Orientalist, Professor E. G. Browne.

He brought to all these undertakings the full impact of his original mind, untrimmed to the wind of other people's opinions of him. He soon felt the inevitable opposition. Plenty of grist could be found for the mill of the jealous and the displaced. There was a custom that the families of deceased professors of Al Azhar received a pension from the university-mosque funds. This was so abused that Mohammed Abdu decided to end it, but so as to make sure that no families with legitimate claims suffered, he saw that they were cared for from a voluntary fund which he organised and largely subscribed to. The idea of social service as a responsibility of fellow citizens loomed large in his mind. He helped to found the Islamic Benevolent Society, to encourage the wealthy to care for the poor and to help educate them. His enemies accused him of using this society for subversive political activities. They complained of this to Lord Cromer, who was in charge of affairs in Egypt, but an investigation cleared him of all such accusations. Between Lord Cromer and Mohammed Abdu there had developed a mutual friendship. It was based on appreciation of many points in each other's character but not mutually on all points.

In 1900 a big fire in the provinces caused great hardship to thousands who were homeless and destitute. The Sheikh used this occasion to organise a relief fund in which he himself went from door to door collecting. This was considered undignified in his position and much criticism arose round the subject. As he would not accept bribes, it was of bribery that he was accused. No proof could here be found, though he once confessed to a young man who offered him a bribe, that he often had to fight temptation hard on that score, for much had been tendered him.

As that accusation failed, baser moves were resorted to and someone produced a fraudulent photograph of the Sheikh in compromising company. Two newspapers also printed a libellous picture of him, for which both owners were eventually condemned to prison sentences.

By now the Khedive Tewfik had died and his son Abbas Hilmi reigned in his stead. On more than one occasion Sheikh Mohammed

Abdu stood up to the latter on matters of principle, and this did not add to his popularity in that quarter.

In between his duties he made time for journeys to Europe. He found these visits very stimulating. There was so much in Europe that he admired and so much of it he longed to give to his own people, that his travels always renewed his hopes and enthusiasm which were at times dimmed by the great difficulties he encountered in Egypt. In the summer of 1903 he and his brother Hamuda visited England, again as the guests of the Blunts. Sheikh Mohammed Abdu had a great desire to meet the old philosopher Herbert Spencer, whose book on education he had translated into Arabic from a French version. It was August and they stayed at Newbuildings Place, the beautiful Sussex country house of the Blunts. They walked together in the woods and spoke of opinions and events, of philosophies and faiths. Mr. Blunt would drive his coach and four (all Arabs) through the Sussex lanes with Mohammed Abdu on the box beside him. The visit was a joy to both.

When they visited Spencer at Brighton, the old man sent his secretary and carriage to meet them at the station. Herbert Spencer was then bed-ridden but most lucid in his mind. He asked the Sheikh whether the main trends of thought in the East were parallel to the ways in which thought was developing in the West. To this Mohammed Abdu replied that more of the evil from the West had been learnt than the good but that wherever thought was deep and inspired then it was the same in East and West. Politics were only spoken of in the widest sense, for, as Harold Spencer wrote of Mohammed Abdu in 1905, "his political outlook was a kind of summons to the war of ideas". The Sheikh also visited Oxford, where he was delighted to find some Arabic manuscripts which were only known by name in Cairo, including the correspondence of an Arab philosopher with Frederick the Great.

During these years the Blunts had a property in Egypt, called Sheikh Obeid, on the edge of the desert a few miles out of Cairo. Mr. Blunt gave Mohammed Abdu an acre of land in the corner of his garden, on which he built a small house. So when the Englishman visited Egypt in the winter he saw much of his Egyptian friend who would drop in for talks on many subjects. It was once to hear a poem of Wilfrid Blunt's explained in Arabic; once to discuss a copy of Butler's *Conquest of Egypt by the Arabs* of which Mohammed Abdu had been sent a presentation copy, and once to report favourably on what he saw of British rule in the Sudan which he had just visited. Another time he looked in to ask that a letter he had written to Tolstoi should be translated, as he thought English a more suitable language in which to send it than Arabic.

There were times, in these his final years, when Mohammed Abdu was tempted to lose faith in humanity, nor did he always feel that the creed of Islam alone could change the ways of man with man. His faith in a Creator and an after-life were undimmed but he admitted in private to agnosticism—to an unknowing—on points of doctrine and of theology.

By 1890 the state of health of Arabi and the exiles in Ceylon again gave cause for anxiety. The certificate signed by three doctors, which was sent to Lord Salisbury, then Foreign Minister, stated that the climate of Ceylon was most unsuitable for Egyptians used to a fine, dry atmosphere. Arabi himself had suffered repeatedly from dysentery, fever and rheumatism. He was said to be in a state of chronic invalidism.

Lord Salisbury instructed the English authorities in Egypt to discover the Khedive's views on whether the prisoners might be transferred to Egypt, there to continue their detention. The Khedive answered that he could not consent to such a scheme "in view of the very bad effect their presence in the country would produce".

In May 1897 three of the exiles sent a long memorial to Queen Victoria in which they stated that they were no longer the active military leaders they had been fifteen years ago, but old men, spirit-broken exiles, only desirous of seeing their beloved children and other relatives whom they had left behind in Egypt when they were exiled.

Their plea was, to be sent as near to Egypt as circumstances would permit. They suggested Cyprus as being a place where their children and grandchildren would be able to visit them occasionally. They pledged their word of honour, as officers and gentlemen, that if they were allowed to live in Cyprus they would still keep their word, and abstain from all interference in political questions.

Arabi did not sign this petition, though in Egypt there was considerable talk about his possible return. Mr. Blunt spoke of it to the Khedive, and some Egyptian army officers hoped it would happen as early as 1889, with the aim of having him form a National Ministry.

It was not till 1901, however, that the exiles' hope began to have some foundation. The Prince of Wales (afterwards King George V), when on a visit to Ceylon, saw and spoke with Arabi. There was no official record of their conversation but it was generally believed that a possible pardon for the exiles was talked about. That same year, Wilfrid Blunt had conversations with Admiral the Hon. Hedworth Lambton who, nineteen years before, had been Flag Lieutenant to Admiral Sir Beauchamp Seymour during the bombardment of Alexandria. Admiral Lambton had seen Arabi in Ceylon in 1898 and was impressed by his bearing. In 1901 Lambton was in command of the Royal Yacht and in direct touch with the Royal Family. This sequel of events might well have brought matters to a head. Arabi received his pardon in May 1901.

His home-coming was quiet and uneventful. No one hailed him except some of the populace, here and there. Boys would still follow him in the street and shout the old cry of twenty years ago, "God give you the victory, O Arabi". But the younger Nationalists of the day looked on him askance for they thought he spoke as if he approved of all that the English had done in Egypt. Neither would Mohammed Abdu meet him at first, for he felt Arabi's views in his old age to be too simple and superficial and that they would harm the true cause of Egypt, sooner or later. It was not long before they did meet, however, and decide to put such differences of opinion to one side. They both came to the Blunts' house outside Cairo. Arabi and Mohammed Abdu embraced when they saw each other; many hours later they were still talking.

In March 1905 Mohammed Abdu went to the Cairo railway station to say good-bye to Wilfrid Blunt who was leaving for England. The Englishman had a premonition that he would not see the Sheikh again, but it was his own death of which Blunt was thinking. Yet Wilfrid Blunt had another seventeen years of life before him, and Mohammed Abdu had but four more months.

He realised that he had been unwell for some time past but was still full of plans, a new paper, the founding of a modern university and an extensive journey to visit Moslems in Persia, India and Russia. The state of his health made him decide first to go to Europe for expert advice and treatment but he did not think more seriously of it than that.

In July he visited a friend in Ramleh near Alexandria for a week's stay before sailing. But here his illness quickly increased. He was in pain and restless. As he lay on his bed the bodily weakness of disease increased rapidly, and it was not long before even the strength to speak left him. All he could murmur was the name of God. From this he seemed to draw comfort. "Allahu akbar" —"God is most great", he would whisper. On 10 July, his wife came and tended him with care and love. As that night went on he was nearly unconscious. His wife could no longer hear what he murmured but she saw his lips move as he formed those words, "God is great". Into these words is poured a wealth of worship by devout Moslems. He was just able to smile at his wife before his courageous spirit left to meet its Creator.

It was on 11 July that he died, of cancer of the liver. The train which bore his body to Cairo stopped at places on the way specially to allow the populace to gather round in respect and in mourning. The funeral prayers were said in Al Azhar but the usual conventional orations of praise were dispensed with for his friends felt them to be out of place when honouring one who had so fought against unreality and had cared so little for the trappings of praise. But the great crowd who mourned him at the cemetery, including Christians, Jews and Moslems, reflected the reality of grief. One man in the crowd was weeping, and as a friend tried to comfort him, he explained that he was not only weeping from his own sadness but for all the poor people to whom it had been his special assignment to distribute a large part of Mohammed Abdu's official salary. "He was great and poor while he lived and poor and great when he died," wrote Sheikh Mustapha Abdul Raziq, one of his Egyptian biographers.

After Mohammed Abdu's visit to Herbert Spencer in 1903 he had jotted down some thoughts in a notebook. "These philosophers and scientists who have discovered so many things that minister to man's comfort. . .are impotent to discover the true nature of man or reveal it to him so that he may know it and turn back to it. These men who burnish crude metal till it becomes bright glittering iron, should it not be easy for them to scour off the rust that covers human nature and to burnish these souls until their spiritual lustre comes back to them?. . . Where is the cure? The return to religion. . .religion reveals men's true nature and makes it known to its possessors in every age but they slide back into ignorance of it."[1]

[1] *Mohammed Abduh*, translated by C. Wendell, op. cit., p. 93.

Ahmed Arabi outlived Mohammed Abdu by six years. He had taken a little house at Helwan, some fifteen miles south of Cairo, and there, on the edge of the desert, he lived very quietly, seeing almost no one except his children and grandchildren to whom he was devoted, though now the pleasure of their companionship was shot through with anxiety for their future. Their cares and misadventures shook him in a way that the threats of Europe had never done.

As years went on, his mental as well as his physical powers became dimmed. An Englishman, Mr. Beaman, who when attached to the British Consulate had known Arabi in his prime, visited him at Helwan a year or two before he died. It was only with difficulty that Mr. Beaman could find anyone able to direct him to Arabi's house, and when he eventually arrived, the old man could hardly remember him, nor recognise one of his own letters written to Mr. Beaman from Ceylon which the latter had brought with him on the visit to show Arabi how carefully it had been kept all those years in token of their friendship.

By September 1911 it became obvious that Arabi was very ill. Two of the best Egyptian doctors attended him and diagnosed cancer. On 19 September an Egyptian friend visited him to offer congratulations on one of the children having gained his primary school certificate. This was a happy occasion.

Arabi's mind roamed over the past during these, his last days, and he would frequently repeat to himself, "It is God who knows that I did not betray my country—I served her—and future generations will recognise this, though the present one denies it."

On 21 September he felt better, and expressed a wish to his family around him for a meal of prawns. Eager to please, someone darted out and bought them, to the horror of the doctors when they heard it. By the evening he was in pain. "When will my release come," he murmured, "will it be after tomorrow? That would be too long to wait." These were his last words.[2]

None but a handful of old friends and relations gathered by his graveside. The young Nationalists of that decade could not understand the particular ways in which his mind and heart had stirred him. They did not comprehend what he had been trying to achieve,

[2] For the above details of Mohammed Abduh and Arabi's last days, see *Ala Firash al Maut*, Tahir Ahmed al Tanahi, Cairo, 1949, and *The Dethronement of the Khedive* by A. H. Beaman, George Allen & Unwin, 1929.

mostly because he had not been allowed to achieve it. Yet, it was they, and the Nationalists who came later, who were the logical outcome of his efforts. And they were also the logical outcome of the treatment accorded to his efforts.

At the time of Arabi's death *The Times* commented on him, "A name. . . which occasioned acute controversy, and events which have had, and may yet have, results of far greater consequence than could then have been anticipated. Probably few characters in themselves so insignificant have ever so largely influenced the history of their times."

Only now, when human wisdom has failed, are people beginning to recognise that the paramount task is to forge in every nation a force of men and women determined to put right what is wrong in themselves and their nations. And in seeking the true destiny of the other nation each nation will find its own.

"Men are hungry for bread, for peace, and for the hope of a new world," says Dr. Frank N. D. Buchman, that great pioneer of world advance. "Before a God-led unity every last problem will be solved. Hands will be filled with work, stomachs with food, and empty hearts with an ideology that really satisfies."[3]

---

[3] *Remaking the World, The Collected Speeches of Dr. Frank Buchman,* Blandford Press, London.

BIBLIOGRAPHY

C. G. ADAMS : *Islam and Modernism in Egypt*. Oxford University Press, 1933.

F. ADAMS : *The New Egypt*. Fisher Unwin, 1907.

AHMED SHAFIQ : *Egypte Moderne et les Influences Etrangéres*. Cairo, 1931.

AMIN YUSEF : *Independent Egypt*. John Murray, 1940.

GEORGE ANTONIUS : *The Arab Awakening*. Hamish Hamilton, 1938.

EDWARD ATIYAH : *The Arabs*. Penguin, 1955.

A. H. BEAMAN : *The Dethronement of the Khedive*. George Allen and Unwin, 1929.

W. BESANT : *The Life and Achievements of E. H. Palmer*. John Murray, 1883.

W. S. BLUNT : *My Diaries 1888-1914*. Martin Secker, 1919.

W. S. BLUNT : *Secret History of the English Occupation of Egypt*. Fisher Unwin, 1907.

W. S. BLUNT : *Gordon at Khartoum*. Stephen Swift, 1912.

A. M. BROADLEY : *How we Defended Arabi and his Friends*. Chapman and Hall, 1884.

E. G. BROWNE : *The Persian Revolution*. Cambridge, 1910.

D. A. CAMERON : *Egypt in the Nineteenth Century*. Smith, Elder, 1878.

SIR V. CHIROL : *The Egyptian Problem*. Macmillan, 1920.

M. COLOMBE : *L'Evolution de l'Egypte*. Paris, 1951.

SIR A. COLVIN : *The Making of Modern Egypt*. Seely & Co., 1906.

THE EARL OF CROMER : *Modern Egypt*. Macmillan 1911, 2nd edition.

E. DICEY : *England and Egypt*. Chapman and Hall, 1881.

E. DICEY : *The Story of the Khedivate*. Rivington, 1902

DUBOIS-RICHARD : *Essai sur les Gouvernement de l'Egypte*. Cairo, 1941.

LT. COL. P. G. ELGOOD : *Egypt*. Arrowsmith, 1935.

LT. COL. P. G. ELGOOD : *The Transit of Egypt*. Edward Arnold, 1928.

C. DE FREYCINET : *La Question d'Egypte*. Paris, 1905.

C. DE FREYCINET : *Souvenirs, 1878-1893*. Paris, 1912.

H. A. R. GIBB : *Modern Trends in Islam*. University of Chicago Press, 1947.

SIR WILLIAM GREGORY : *An Autobiography*. John Murray, 1894.

M. G. HANOTAUX AND SHEIKH MOHAMMED ABDU : *L'Europe et l'Islam*. Cairo, 1905.

J. HEYWORTH-DUNNE : *An Introduction to the History of Education in Modern Egypt*. Luzac, 1939.

J. HEYWORTH-DUNNE : *Religious and Political Trends in Modern Egypt*. Washington, 1948.

J. C. HUREWITZ : *Diplomacy in the Near and Middle East*. Macmillan, 1957.

C. ISSAWI : *Egypt at Mid-Century*. Oxford University Press, 1954.

C. ISSAWI *Khedives and Pashas : By one who knew them well*. Sampson Low, 1884.

JAMAL MOHAMMED AHMED : *The Intellectual Origins of Egyptian Nationalism*. Oxford University Press, 1960.

BARON DE KUSEL : *An Englishman's Recollections of Egypt*. Bodley Head, 1915.

180 BIBLIOGRAPHY

J. & S. LACOUTURE : *Egypt in Transition*. Methuen, 1958.

J. LANDAU : *Parliamentary Parties in Egypt*. Tel Aviv, 1953.

W. LAQUEUR : *Communism and Nationalism in the Middle East*. Wiedenfeld and Nicolson, 1956.

T. LITTLE : *Egypt*. Benn, 1958.

C. CHAILLÉ LONG : *The Three Prophets*. New York, 1884.

LORD LLOYD : *Egypt Since Cromer*. Macmillan, 1933.

SIR E. MALET : *Egypt 1879-1883*. John Murray, 1909.

J. MARLOWE : *Anglo-Egyptian Relations, 1880-1953*. Cresset Press, 1954.

VISCOUNT MILNER : *England in Egypt*. Edward Arnold, 1909.

MOHAMMED ABDU : *Rissalat al Tawhid*. Translated by B. Michel and Sheikh Ali Abdul Raziq, Paris, 1925.

MOHAMMED NEGUIB : *Egypt's Destiny*. Gollanz, 1950.

MOHAMMED RIFAAT : *The Awakening of Modern Egypt*. Longmans, 1947.

MOHAMMED SABRY : *La Genése de l'Esprit National d'Egypte*. Paris, 1924.

J. MORLEY : *The Life of William Ewart Gladstone*. Vol. III. Macmillan, 1903.

E. W. POLSON NEWMAN : *Great Britain in Egypt*. Cassell, 1928.

H. Z. NUSEIBEH : *The Ideas of Arab Nationalism*. New York, 1956.

J. NINET : *Arabi Pasha*. The Author. Berne, 1884.

OSMAN AMIN : *Muhammad Abduh*. Translated by C. Wendell. Washington, 1953.

C. ROYLE : *Egyptian Campaigns, 1882-1885*. Hurst and Blackett, 1886.

N. SCOTIDIS : *L'Egypte Contemporaine et Arabi Pasha*. Paris, 1888.

W. CANTWELL SMITH : *Islam in Modern History*. New York, 1957.

H. VILLIERS STUART : *Egypt after the War*. John Murray, 1883.

M. TRAVERS SYMONS : *The Riddle of the Sphinx*. Frank Palmer.

D. MCKENZIE WALLACE : *Egypt and the Egyptian Question*. Macmillan, 1883.

V. SETON WILLIAMS. *Britain and the Arab States*. Luzac, 1948.

G. WINT and P. CALVOCORESSI : *Middle East Crisis*. Penguin, 1957.

J. A. WYLIE : *Egypt and its Future*. Edinburgh.

G. YOUNG : *Egypt*. Benn, 1927.

PAMPHLETS

A. A. ATEEK : *Al Azhar, the University and Mosque*. Egypt Education Bureau, London.

ALEXANDER BAIRD : *The Egyptian Muddle*. William Blackwood, 1884.

H. R. FOX BOURNE : *Political Institutions in Egypt*. Notes on Egyptian Affairs No. 3. 1907.

The Egyptian National Claims. Memorandum presented by the Egyptian Delegation to the Peace Conference. London, 1919.

LADY GREGORY : *Arabi and his Household*. Kegan Paul, 1884.

LT. COL. HENNEBERT : *The English in Egypt*. Translated by B. Pauncefoote. W. H. Allen, 1884.

J. SEYMOUR KEAY : *Spoiling the Egyptians*. Kegan Paul, 1882.

REV. J. HOLLOWELL : *The Financial Tyranny in Egypt under the Conservatives*. Nottingham, 1884.

CAPITAINE MERA : *Une Page de Politique Coloniale.* Paris, 1913.
MOHAMMED FAHMY : *La Verite sur la Question d'Egypte.* Geneva, 1913.

ARABIC TEXTS

DR. ABDUL HAMID AL BATRIK : *Tarikh Misr fi al Asr al Hadith.* Cairo, 1954.
ABDUL RAHMAN AL RAFI'I : *Al Thaurat al Arabiyah wa al Ihtilal al Inglizi.* Cairo, 1937.
AHMED SHAFIQ : *Mudhakkirati fi Nisf Qurn.* Cairo, 1934.
JURJI ZAIDAN : *Tarajim Mashahir al Sharq.* Cairo, 1910.
MOHAMMED ABDU : *Al Islam wa al Nasraniyat ma al ilm wa al Madaniyat.* Cairo, 1938. 5th Edition.
MOHAMMED RASHID RIDA : *Tarikh....al Sheikh Mohammed Abdu.* Vols. I and III. Cairo, 1906.
MUSTAPHA ABDUL RAZIQ : *Mohammed Abdu.* Cairo, 1946.
OSMAN AMIN : *Mohammed Abdu.* Cairo, 1944.
QADRI QALAJI : *Mohammed Abdu.* Batal al Thaurat al fikriyah fi al Islam. Beirut, 1948.
TAHIR AHMED AL TANAHI : *Ala Firash al Maut.* Cairo, 1949.

INDEX

ABBAS HILMI, KHEDIVE, 173
Abbasi, Sheikh al, 26
Abbassia, 145
Abdin Barracks, 55
Abdin Palace 30, 53ff., 145ff., 153
Abdin Square, 54, 146
Abyassinia, 38, 39
Admiralty, 91, 95, 120, 124, 137
Africa, North, 166
Ahmed Arabi, 3, 4; youth, 36; joins the army, 37; in Abyssinia, 38; in disgrace, 39ff; punished, 41ff; joins National Party, 46ff; further grievances, 48, 49; leads revolt, 50, 51; challenges the Khedive, 53; works with Mohammed Abdul, 55; transferred, 56 interview with Mr. Colvin, 58; meets Mr. Blunt, 59; Undersecretary for War, 62; Minister for War, 64; described by Col. Long, 66; quarrels with Khedive, 71ff; writes to Mr. Blunt, 74; varied English opinions of him, 75; meets Mr. Cornish, 87; visits Waterworks, 88; answers Darwish Pasha, 94; meets with Khedive, 95; at Kafr al Dawar, 111, 112; his cause upheld by noble ladies, 112; summoned by Khedive, 114; re Suez Canal, 120; called a rebel, 118, 129; interviews Midshipman de Chair, 131; his troops, 132; withdraws to Tel al Kebir, 134; taken prisoner, 145ff; suggestions for his punishment, 149; Messrs. Broadley and Napier to defend him, 150, 151; treatment in prison, 152ff; pre-arranged verdict, 155, 156; trial, 157ff; exiled, 159ff; in Ceylon, 168ff; pardoned, 175; his death, 177, 178
Ahmed Khan, Sayed, 3

Ahmed Minshawi Bey, 112
Ahmedi Mosque, 14, 15, 19, 27
Ahram, Al, 24
Alexandra, H. M. S., 98, 131
Alexandra, Princess, 131
Alexandria, 6, 9, 29, 30, 41, 53, 57, 72, 77, 79ff, 85, 89, 90, 93, 95, 98, 104, 106ff, 112, 114, 150, 175
Alexandria, Governor of, 100, 111
Algiers, 137
Ali Sadik, 72
Alison, Maj. Gen. Sir A., 111
Allen, Capt., 107
America, 33, 39, 41, 66, 91, 92, 101, 105, 159 (see also United States)
American officers, 38
Anti-Aggression League, 85, 86
Arabi (see Ahmed)
Arabi, Madame, 64, 65, 168
Austria, 77, 121, 126, 130
Azhar, Al, 9, 19ff, 22ff, 31, 36, 38, 73, 78, 111, 114, 172, 176

BADGER, THE REV. DR., 69
Baker, Sir Samuel, 68
Bakhor, 139, 141
Bank of Egypt, 9, 107
Baring, Mr. W., 123
Bateman, Mr., 10, 11, 13
Beaman, Mr., 177
Bedouin, 96, 97, 103, 114, 131, 137ff, 145
Beirut, 89, 106, 163, 166, 167, 170
Beirut, Mayor of, 167
Bell, Mr. Moberley, 39, 153
Beni Suef, 33
Bennett, Mr. J. G., 133
Berne, 149
Besant, Mr. W., 138
Biblioteque Nationale de Paris, 46
Bilbeis, 145
Bismark, Prince, 47
Blonfield, N., 127

39437